EFFECTIVE AND ACCOUNTABLE POLICING

Ideas for Effective Police Reform

Second Edition

About the Author

Marlin Price began his law enforcement career with the Dallas Police Department as a patrol officer in 1972. Rising quickly through the ranks he became Assistant Chief of Police in 1988. During his tenure with the Dallas Police Department, he commanded the Professional Standards Bureau, two Patrol Operations Divisions, the Special Investigations Division, and the Criminal Investigations Bureau. In 2000, after 28 years and 12 years as an Assistant Chief, Chief Price retired from Dallas and accepted the position of Chief of Police in Southlake, Texas. Chief Price served the City of Southlake for almost five years before retiring in 2005.

Chief Price, an Assessor and Team Leader for the Commission on Accreditation for Law Enforcement, was recruited by the Texas Police Chiefs Association in 2006 to develop an Accreditation Program for Texas cities. He developed and coordinated the Texas Law Enforcement Accreditation Program until his retirement in 2014. Chief Price continues to serve Texas law enforcement by teaching chiefs and command officers around the state for the Texas Police Chiefs Association. His classes include Managing Patrol Operations, Managing Criminal Investigations, as well as Auditing and Inspections. Chief Price has also conducted audits and reviews of police department operations for the Texas Police Chiefs Association and has completed over 60 operational reviews of police departments across Texas.

Chief Price has a Bachelor's degree in Criminal Justice and a Master's degree in Public Administration. He is a graduate of the 135th Session of the FBI National Academy and a graduate of the Southwestern Law Enforcement Institute's Command and Management College. He is also a graduate of the Police Executive Research Forum's Senior Management Institute for Police at the Kennedy School of Government. .

EFFECTIVE AND ACCOUNTABLE POLICING

Ideas for Effective Police Reform

Chief Marlin Price, (Ret.) B.S., M.P.A.
Southlake, Texas, Chief of Police (Retired)
Dallas, Texas, Assistant Chief (Retired)
Texas Police Chiefs Association, Accreditation Program
Director (Retired)

Second Edition

EFFECTIVE AND ACCOUNTABLE POLICING
Ideas for Effective Police Reform

Second Edition

Published in the United States of America
© Chief Marlin Price, (Ret.) B.S., M.P.A
8200 Olympia Drive
McKinney, Texas 75072

Copyright ©2023
ISBN: 979-8-9881371-2-2 (paper)
ISBN: 979-8-9881371-3-9 (eBook)
Library of Congress Control Number: 2023920784

Cover and formatting by 341 Enterprise

Acknowledgments

Throughout my career, I have worked for many different police chiefs. While some were good, even exceptional, some were much less than desirable. Most police officers I have worked with have been wonderful, dedicated, honest, and fair police officers, supervisors, and managers. From the depths of my heart, I want to thank those men and women with whom I have worked, and those whom I have never met for the work they did, and for the work they continue to do.

Everyone with whom I have worked influenced me. The good ones made me think, "I want to be like that!" The bad ones provided me with a clear understanding of what I did not want to be. Thank you to all of you who played a positive role model during my career.

Finally, I want to extend my sincere thanks to former Dallas Police Chief Ben Click, who came to Dallas from the Phoenix Police Department. He is still the best police chief I have ever known and provided me with a wonderful model. He was kind enough to review this book and provide valuable feedback, which I truly treasure.

Thank you, Ben!

VI

Introduction

With fifty years in law enforcement operations, thirty-three as a uniformed sworn officer from street officer to chief, and seventeen years working as a non-sworn police manager and state accreditation program director – I have developed a deep understanding of the problems facing modern policing. As an accreditation program director comparing police agencies' operations to the best practices of the day, it has become increasingly clear that many mayors, city council members, city managers, school superintendents, university presidents, and even some police chiefs have little understanding of what police agencies can and should be doing. They lack important information to know if they are doing their job effectively and constitutionally, and how many officers are needed to do so. Many police departments continue to function the same way they always have simply because no one initiates change. No one demands accountability or efficiency because they don't know what *can* be done or how it can be improved.

Policing has changed significantly over the past fifty years and will continue to change at an increasing rate over the next fifty. The level of training and technology used in addressing crime and community order has exploded. But even with our training and technological advances, we still can't seem to get it right. Calls for police reform and accountability have echoed through our cities. And we can no longer accept the status quo.

Today, we have some of the most intelligent and competent police chiefs in the history of policing, but many fail to carry through with their mission either through a lack of ability, knowledge, or direction. Still, others were great when they started, but now are just waiting for retirement and hoping nothing bad happens. Additionally, some have only worked for mediocre chiefs in the past and may not understand that there are better ways. Allowing a police agency (even with an extremely competent chief) to function without oversight and accountability allows for poor outcomes and in some cases outright disaster. City managers, school superintendents, and university presidents are often timid in demanding improved performance from their police agency because they are not police experts. They often don't know what can or cannot be done given current staffing or legal constraints. Most systems of civilian oversight like Civilian Review Boards lack any credible authority. But city managers, mayors, councils, superintendents, and school boards are civilians, and they have all the authority they need – but many just don't know what can be done, or simply fail to do it.

I have developed the belief that cities, school districts, colleges and universities, and other organizations get the police departments they deserve – or basically what they accept. The leadership of the police chief is critical, but ultimate leadership in most organizations comes from an elected or appointed council or board, through a city manager or administrator, down to the police chief. The council or board holds the ultimate responsibility for the operation of an organization. They delegate responsibility to the top administrator, but they need to be asking questions to ensure their desires are carried out. The same goes for the administrator in delegating responsibility to a police chief.

A city's public safety and education system is critical to economic development. People and corporations are not going to invest in a city where their families are not safe and where there are poor educational opportunities. Proper management and accountability of a police department are therefore crucial to any city's growth. And, all citizens must recognize that there is a cost to quality policing.

This handbook is intended to be a quick and easy read about police operations for those responsible for ensuring a safe city, school district, university, or other organization. The views expressed here are mine alone, although admittedly I have been influenced significantly by scientific research and my association with some of the best police professionals in this business. It also comes from seeing some of our country's worst policing mistakes – most of which were preventable. Police departments must become more effective in their efforts at crime control, while at the same time, they must become more accountable to their communities. We will discuss both issues in the pages that follow.

City councils, boards, and organizations have the ultimate right to determine, within the law, what they want their police departments to do. If it is not what the citizens, students, or shareholders want, the council or board will end up being replaced (in theory of course). As much as I disliked the Council and Manager telling me - the police chief -what they wanted done or asking questions about what was being done, that is exactly what needed to occur. I intend to make this understanding clearer while helping both police chiefs and organizational leaders build better relationships – all leading to greater police *accountability*.

While writing this handbook, I had municipal police operations in mind. School and university boards of trustees, superintendents and presidents, and other organizations may find it helpful in transferring these ideas to their organizations. Setting goals, monitoring activities, periodic reporting, auditing and inspecting operations, asking questions, and holding their police agency accountable for achieving goals are basic to *all* policing organizations. School and university policing has changed in recent years, moving from campus crime control to the protection of students and faculty. Unfortunately, there has not been a great deal of academic research on the best methods of carrying out these goals or staffing these agencies. In addition to ensuring officers are available, it is crucial that they also be professionally trained and equipped, to be able to respond when students and faculty are present. They also need to be given clear instructions on what is expected of them.

Throughout this book, I express a need for council members or other board members to request data, ask questions, or investigate policing strategies for themselves. Of course, this can easily irritate any city manager, superintendent, or police chief, often causing extra work. Council members must allow the city manager to manage the municipal operation, as well as be aware of the extra work these questions create. All requests for data or answers to questions should be fielded through the city manager for a response. The manager should be advised of any direct questions put to employees as well as the employees' responses.

All visits to city departments should be coordinated by the city manager. However, the ultimate responsibility for the operations of a police department rests squarely with the city manager and council. Requiring the police department to investigate issues of concern, make periodic reports, or conduct audits may force police agencies to see data that they may not have seen or understood before. This will allow them to take the necessary actions to fix any problems. No longer is it acceptable to say, "We didn't know." This attitude does not reflect responsibility or accountability.

I do not expect all my former colleagues, current chiefs, or city managers, and council members to agree with me, as I am sure some will not. But I do hope these discussions will inspire continued debate, study, and experimentation to better protect our future generations.

Table of Contents

Chapter 1
A Brief History of Policing in the United States

Early Policing Efforts

Crime and disorder have been with us for a very long time. Historically, while crime may not have been clearly defined in statutes, behavior that offended the sensibilities of the majority has been punished in some form or another. The first form of policing in America was the "night watch" created in Boston in the 1630s. The night watch was originally hired by the townspeople, but this job eventually became the responsibility of the city government. Unfortunately, many of these city officials and police officers were corrupt and ineffective. Those citizens who were rich enough would hire private individuals to function as guards to protect their persons, family, or property.

From these early roots, law enforcement and crime control developed in a multitude of ways around the country – from slave patrols in the South to sheriffs and frontier marshals in the West. With the influx of immigrants in the early 1800s and the conflicts they created, larger cities began to realize they needed a more formal way to keep order, leading to the first police department formed in Boston in 1838. New York City followed shortly thereafter in 1845.

These first police departments supposedly were developed along the lines of the British Metropolitan Police, formed as a result of Sir Robert Peel's Metropolitan Police Act of 1829. Peel's approach was to prevent crime *before* it occurred, versus focusing on catching criminals. Peel's Nine Policing Principles was a great step forward in policing and is still relevant today. Unfortunately, politicians at the time tended to use the police to meet their political ends. Hence, corruption reigned in most police agencies. This corruption continued until the early 1900s when a few agencies began to reform their police departments.

While Sir Robert Peel (Prime Minister in England in the early 19th century) is known as the father of modern policing, it is August Vollmer (the first Police Chief of Berkley, California in 1909) who is known as the father of American policing. Vollmer advocated higher education for police officers and instituted many needed reforms and policing innovations, such as fingerprint-ing and centralized records systems. O.W. Wilson, also known as the father of the law enforcement code of ethics, was strongly influenced by Vollmer. Wil-son became a Police Commissioner for Chicago, then the Dean at Berkley. He also wrote a police textbook on police organization and management, which is still in use in some places today. In this textbook, Wilson advocated for creat-ing a "police omnipresence," consisting of random preventive patrol and rapid response to calls. He believed that taking this approach would make criminals fearful of being caught, which would then deter future crimes.

Police reforms continued to occur up through the 1950s and 1960s. It is interesting to note that during this era, a good cop was expected to provide street corner justice through persuasion, threats, and even physical force to keep order. This was done to keep the number of individuals in the formal court and prison system to a minimum. These ideas began to disappear with our new liti-gious society.

Wilson's theory of omnipresence pervaded the thinking of police agen-cies and administrators for decades, until the introduction of critical police re-search beginning in the 1970s. The 1960s in America were filled with racial tension, and civil rights riots were occurring across the nation. In 1965, Presi-dent Johnson created the President's Commission on Law Enforcement and the Administration of Justice. The Commission comprised 19 members including lawyers, judges, prosecutors, police officials, and citizens. The Commission is-sued 16 publications, the most important of which was the "Challenge of Crime in a Free Society." This document outlined a myriad of much-needed changes in policing and the administration of justice. It also spawned a new era of scien-tific research into police operations and practices.

One of the first major studies conducted was the Kansas City Preventive Patrol Study (1973). This study was evaluated by the Police Foundation, now named the National Policing Institute. The study tested the basic idea of random preventive patrol. Scientifically designed, the study tested whether random pre-ventive patrol impacted arrests, crime control, or citizen satisfaction. The study found that the amount of random preventive patrol did not affect any of the outcomes. This study has been replicated numerous times in other cities with the same result. We will discuss this study later in the book (**Chapter 6**), but it was clear that the idea of police omnipresence does not work. Other subsequent studies on how policing can be more effective with fewer resources continue today.

With these scientifically designed studies, we are now beginning to see what works to reduce crime -- and what does *not* work. In recent years, the most significant proposed changes come from the President's Commission on 21st Century Policing. This Commission (similar to President Johnson's commission in the '60s) was formed after the death of Michael Brown in Ferguson, Missouri, and the resulting protests. The final report of this Commission was issued in May 2015 and had six major pillars. The first was building trust between the police and the community through the implementation and use of procedural justice.

21st Century Policing

The 21st Century Policing report is available online for free as a PDF. The executive summary, while only four pages long, offers an excellent summary of the Commission's findings. The report built its recommendations on six major topics or pillars, which are:

Building Trust & Legitimacy
Policy & Oversight
Technology & Social Media
Community Policing & Crime Control
Training & Education
Officer Wellness & Safety

While these pillars all contain valid and needed recommendations, building trust and legitimacy has received the most national attention. The Commission stated, "Building trust and nurturing legitimacy on both sides of the police/ citizen divide is the foundational principle underlying the nature of relations between law enforcement agencies and the communities they serve. Decades of research and practice support the premise that people are more likely to obey the law when they believe that those who are enforcing the law are perceived to have the legitimate authority to do so. The public confers legitimacy only on those whom they believe are acting in procedurally just ways."

Procedural justice incorporates the following four principles:

Treat people with dignity and respect. Clearly convey respect during an encounter and show that you empathize with their concerns and points of view.

Give individuals a voice during encounters. Let the involved individuals tell their story completely during an encounter.

Be neutral and transparent in your decision-making. Do this regardless of how you may personally feel.

Convey a trustworthy motive. Explain, whenever possible, the reasons for your decisions and the actions taken.

As a result of the task force report, many agencies around the country have adopted the procedural justice model and trained their officers in procedural justice techniques. Reports from these agencies in professional publications indicate increased success in improving community relations both in individual encounters and in the community at large.

Possible Questions for the Police Department

1. Does the department train and practice procedural justice?

2. What specific actions is the department taking to build better relationships with our community?

Chapter 2
Politics, Policing Options and Costs

There are few things worse than a discussion of politics that will cause a reader to stop reading. But politics does influence policing. And we must understand the impact of political beliefs on policing in a community. While city governments rarely embrace the Republican/Democratic identifications, the underlying beliefs of police organizations, city management, and elected leaders do have a significant influence on police operations and activities.

People's political beliefs, whether conservative or liberal, are formed over their lifetime beginning in childhood with their parents, their friends, and teachers influencing the development of their beliefs. Child psychologists believe that these beliefs, once established in the early teen years, become very difficult to change. Conservatives today place a high value on personal responsibility. While everyone wants lawful behavior and social order, conservatives often see every violation of the law as needing strict enforcement. They often believe every crime is an individual choice and if you choose to violate the law, you deserve the appropriate punishment. Clearly, this is a generality and many conservatives have a much less rigid belief system. This conservative belief system was the primary belief system in the initial development of what we will call traditional policing.

Police chiefs seldom come from outside the police profession. The vast majority come up through the ranks, learning the intricacies of the work. As a generalization, most young police officers are very conservative and often very black and white in their view of the world. They often believe that you shouldn't do the crime if you can't do the time. Things are very simple, the law is the right way to behave and if you choose not to do so, then you deserve to go to jail. They believe heavily in the personal responsibility model of behavior. There is seldom any influence within policing that works to change or modify this belief system and our police chiefs are usually drawn from this pool of police candidates. The role models most new chiefs have experienced have been from this same very traditional policing model. However, many of these chiefs are still very effective if they are using effective techniques and work in a conservative community.

Traditional versus Progressive Policing

Traditional policing practices have long centered around a model of law enforcement that emphasizes maintaining order through a focus on enforcement of the law through arrests and prosecution and reactive response to crimes. This approach typically involves a strong police presence in communities, with officers primarily tasked with responding to emergencies and enforcing laws. This approach tends to prioritize arrests and convictions as measures of success, potentially leading to the over-policing of certain neighborhoods, particularly those with marginalized populations. Critics argue that this model can perpetuate systemic racism and disproportionately impact communities of color.

On the other hand, more progressive policing practices aim to shift the focus from a purely punitive approach to one that prioritizes community engagement, problem-solving, and prevention. Community-oriented policing, for example, seeks to build trust and collaboration between police officers and the communities they serve. This approach involves officers working closely with community members to identify and address the root causes of crime, rather than simply responding to incidents after they occur. By involving community stakeholders in the decision-making process, progressive policing practices aim to tailor solutions to the specific needs and concerns of each neighborhood.

Another key difference lies in the use of force and de-escalation techniques. Progressive policing encourages officers to prioritize communication and conflict resolution, resorting to force only as a last resort. This contrasts with traditional policing, where officers might default to forceful tactics in potentially volatile situations. De-escalation training is a cornerstone of progressive approaches, emphasizing techniques that can help prevent unnecessary violence and protect both officers and civilians.

Furthermore, transparency and accountability are central components of progressive policing. This includes mechanisms for civilian oversight, body-worn cameras, and clear guidelines for officer conduct. By fostering transparency, police departments can rebuild trust within the communities they serve, addressing concerns about abuse of power and misconduct. In contrast, the traditional model might sometimes resist such changes, viewing them as threats to the established order.

Differences in Traditional and Progressive police agencies.

Approach to Community Engagement: In a traditional police department, community engagement might be limited to occasional meetings or events. The department relies on answering calls and making arrests to control crime. In a progressive police department, community engagement is a central focus, with officers actively working to build trust and collaborate with community members through ongoing dialogue and partnerships. They are more likely to use scientifically proven methods for preventing crime before it happens.

Problem-Solving Emphasis: Traditional policing often focuses on reacting to crimes after they occur. Progressive policing places a greater emphasis on proactive problem-solving, aiming to identify and address the underlying causes of crime and prevent offenses before they occur.

Use of Force Philosophy: Progressive police departments prioritize de-escalation and non-violent conflict resolution techniques. Traditional departments might rely more heavily on forceful tactics and do not prioritize de-escalation techniques.

Hierarchy and Decision-Making: Traditional police departments often operate within a strict hierarchical structure, where decisions come from the top down. Progressive departments might adopt a more collaborative and inclusive decision-making process, involving officers at various ranks and community members.

Internal Operations: Traditional police agencies seldom conduct internal analysis of systems and often evaluate and promote members that uphold traditional values. Progressive departments take the initiative to conduct internal analyses to determine effectiveness and community satisfaction. They also rely less on arrest or citation numbers in personnel evaluations and value and promote those that demonstrate alternative problem-solving.

Accountability and Transparency: Progressive police departments place a strong emphasis on transparency, utilizing tools like body-worn cameras and improved technology to hold officers accountable for their actions. Traditional departments might have more limited transparency measures in place.

Training Emphasis: Progressive police departments invest in training that covers not only law enforcement skills but also cultural sensitivity, de-escalation techniques, implicit bias, and communication skills. Traditional departments might prioritize technical training without a focus on interpersonal skills.

Metrics of Success: Traditional police departments often measure success in terms of arrest rates and crime statistics. Progressive departments consider a broader range of metrics, including community satisfaction, reduction in repeat offenses, and improved social outcomes.

Diversity and Inclusion: Progressive police departments actively seek to diversify their ranks to reflect the communities they serve. Traditional departments might have less emphasis on diversity and struggle with representation.

Resource Allocation: Traditional departments may allocate resources predominantly to law enforcement activities.

Response to Mental Health Issues Progressive police departments develop specialized training to handle mental health crises with empathy and appropriate interventions. Traditional departments may lack such specialized training and may rely more on forceful interventions in such situations.

It's important to note that these differences exist on a spectrum, and not all traditional or progressive police departments will fit neatly into these categories. Many police agencies are evolving and adapting their practices over time to align with more progressive approaches that prioritize community well-being and equitable justice.

Over the last two decades, we have seen many communities becoming more progressive in their understanding of crime and the criminal justice system. In response to some of the most horrendous policing errors, citizens across the country are questioning policing decisions as never before. In response to these new demands from communities, we are seeing a new breed of more progressive police chiefs in many of these communities. These communities are usually larger cities where the populations are more liberal and tend to value equal opportunity, social programs, and assistance to those in need instead of arrests and punishment. New like-minded police chiefs in these cities are changing the face of policing.

Neither of these positions is mutually exclusive, however. You will often find some very good traditional police chiefs doing very progressive things. And you will often find more progressive police departments holding on to some very traditional policies and practices. Every department is different. Citizens don't often understand that. Communities will build and maintain the police department they want. If a small rural Oklahoma town that is 98 percent conservative wants a traditional police department, that is what the city will have. These political issues are discussed here to remind those evaluating a police department that not all departments have to be alike, with the same policies. Clearly, some very honorable and dedicated people want all police agencies to change and be more progressive right now, and that is the rub. As long as different city councils have different views of how our police agencies must operate, we will not likely achieve that goal anytime soon.

State law and court decisions define what police officers can legally do.

With that understanding, police departments' operations still vary significantly between cities based on the preferences of their city management and council, as well as the education, training, values, and beliefs of their police chief. Some of these differences stem from the views of the political beliefs of their council and community.

Some of the more vocal advocates for change want the criminal justice system to eliminate the "systemic racism" inherent in the system. There is no doubt from the statistics that we have more African Americans in prison nationwide than their percentage in the population. Some can argue that they commit more crimes. However, there is evidence that the system itself does impact them at a greater rate. Why is that?

There is no doubt that the misdemeanor criminal system has a greater impact on minorities and the poor than it does on those who can afford attorneys and bail. No one from either side of the aisle believes that people who murder, rape, assault, rob, loot, or clearly endanger the public should not be arrested and punished, even if the crime is a misdemeanor and even if the offender is a minority. But an arrest for many of our minor "order maintenance" crimes such as loitering, begging, sleeping in public, camping, and even many of our non-hazardous traffic violations such as a broken tail light or no license plate light can have a devastating impact on those who live in poverty.

Some conservatives will say it is still a choice to commit a crime or not, and that is true. It does come down to a choice. But liberals and those advocating for reform of "systemic racism" see the outcomes of those choices are much different between rich and poor. The Federal Reserve Board conducts an economic well-being survey every year. In 2022, the survey found that 37 percent of Americans would have significant difficulty in coming up with $400 in emergency cash. Eighteen percent of Americans have less than $100 in savings.

First, there is little chance that a rich person would ever be arrested for shoplifting. Their choice was to purchase the item or steal it. They had the money to purchase it, but they decided to steal it instead. If they were caught, they would likely have the money to immediately bond out of jail, and hire an attorney, and if the worst happened and they were convicted, they would likely get probation. They would have the money to pay the court costs and probation fees, ending up with maybe a $1,000 to $2,500 dent in their savings. A poor person did make the same choice as well, but the outcome of those choices was paying for the item or stealing it and keeping the little money they had to pay the rent or food for the kids. The options and choices were much different.

Certainly, being poor does not justify more serious felony crimes or looting stores during protests, but police officers are usually very good at determining when lower-income people acted out of desperation. Those who have the good fortune to have had good parents, an education, and encouragement can get good-paying jobs and most often can live within their means. But in this example, the poor would likely end up staying in jail, possibly losing their job, possibly being evicted from their home, and kids having to transfer to a relative's school district. With no money to pay for an attorney to represent them, they may have to take the only option available to get out of jail – pleading guilty. Now with a record, they may lose any federal or state financial aid, be unable to get a good-paying job, and possibly even get deported. Some conservatives may believe this is the natural order of things, and liberals see this more as inequality. The debate is not likely to be solved by reading this book, but understanding the sides of the issue may foster calmer and more realistic discussions. Because minorities make up a larger portion of the lower classes, often because of past discrimination, they are usually impacted by the misdemeanor system at a much greater rate. While this is an example of what many term "systemic racism," in reality it is more economic discrimination than we like to believe.

Once again, neither traditional nor progressive police departments are intrinsically better than the other any more than we can say conservatives are better than liberals – as we all have our own view of the world. But what we are seeing is a significant shift in all parts of our country to more progressive policing. If your city is becoming more liberal or progressive, **Chapter 8** identifies some strategies that departments can use to move in that direction.

The hiring, training, and retaining of police officers is an extremely expensive process. This is no surprise to those who have gone through their first city budget session. An officer's salary and benefits package can run from $100,000 in rural areas to well over $140,000 in urban areas. The equipment provided to an individual officer can cost as much as $20,000. Add another $15,000 for training. A fully equipped police vehicle can cost as much as $100,000.

Hiring a police officer also takes time. It usually takes months for testing and background investigations. All states have some form of state-mandated minimum requirements for to hiring and training police officers. This training can range up to nine months in an academy, with another six months of field training under the wing of experienced senior officers. Fielding a fully trained officer can take as long as 18 months in many agencies. Even when fully trained and released from field training, new officers may need several more months before they become sufficiently self-confident in their role and begin to take personal initiative in their activities. To reduce this training cost and delay, many agencies actively recruit trained and experienced officers from other agencies.

All cities struggle with properly financing their police departments. Police unions and associations are always asking for more money for their officers. Even if a city agrees to give these raises, it becomes quite clear that continuing to give significant raises across the board may be unsustainable. Some cities, however, have found innovative ways to make policing more sustainable. They do this by regionalizing policing activities. Examples include smaller cities contracting with other cities for full-policing services (eliminating administrative overhead), sharing the cost of dispatch, jail, investigative units, and others including animal control operations. Oftentimes, improvements in employee benefits can be more sustainable than salary.

So, what should our police department and our officers be doing? Since President Johnson's Crime Commission report in 1967, agencies across our country have engaged in scientific experiments to help figure out the answer. Scientific means well planned experiments, that detailed records were kept, and partnering with universities and academicians to properly and independently evaluate their programs. The agencies also sought peer review and the replication of the experiment in other cities. The 1970s and 1980s were the golden era of policing experimentation, but it continues to this day.

We are all aware that crime occurs for a myriad of reasons and police can affect only a small portion of these crimes. There is no doubt, however, that crime would be much higher if the police were not available to respond. While the police have little ability to stop a spontaneous individual assault inside a family residence, there are things that police can do to reduce or prevent some crimes before they occur. Once an individual realizes that the police routinely respond to crimes with the intent of arresting the offenders, it may help to restrain an abusive partner. Counseling a crime victim, and in some cases the offender, after an assault may prevent further assaults and injuries. Unfortunately, many of the broader crime prevention ideas of the social scientists in the 1970s and 1980s, such as changing the social fabric of a neighborhood, are far beyond the control of police or even cities to accomplish.

Again, what should our police department and our officers be doing? One of the most influential individuals in modern policing was Herman Goldstein. He was professor emeritus at the University of Wisconsin-Madison Law School and the original architect of the problem-oriented approach to policing. In 1977, Professor Goldstein identified several traditional goals for police departments. These goals include:

- Prevent and control conduct widely recognized as threatening to life and property, which are considered serious crimes.

- Aid individuals who are in danger of physical harm, such as the victim of a criminal attack.

- Protect constitutional guarantees, such as the right to free speech and assembly.

- Facilitate the movement of people and vehicles, such as managing crosswalks and traffic jams.

- Assist those who cannot care for themselves. These include those who are intoxicated, addicted, mentally ill, physically disabled, and the old and very young.

- Resolve conflict, whether between individuals, groups of individuals or individuals and their government.

- Identify problems that have the potential for becoming more serious problems for individual citizens, the police or government.

- Create and maintain a sense of security in the community.

- Build public trust in the police by increasing legitimacy through developing partnerships with the community, which reduces crime and disorder, and increases security.

Over time it appears that police departments in America have paid the most attention to only the first two of the above goals. The American public has been conditioned to call 911 for any emergency they encounter. If they "see something," they need to "say something." Police agencies have increasingly become slaves to the 911 system and have little time left for crime prevention and community policing activities. Agencies throughout our country have seen a loss of staff due to the negative portrayal of police in recent years (albeit some well-deserved). This short staffing has led agencies to move staff from crime prevention and community services to patrol in order to maintain quick call response times that citizens demand.

The first decision cities must make is to decide if they just want a traditional police department that just answers calls and arrests as many violators as possible, or do they want a department that works to prevent crimes from occurring in the first place.

But the basic question remains, "Can police impact crime in a community if they have sufficient resources?" The answer is an enthusiastic *yes, but....* The *but* requires the actions below. In the past few decades, policing has developed methods of impacting and reducing crime -- but many agencies are unaware of these strategies, or simply find it easier to simply answer service calls and report whatever crimes were identified through these calls. Instead, the community should be doing the following:

1. Hire a competent police chief who is aware of the programs that work in policing.

2. Train willing supervisors and commanders in the techniques to reduce crime and require them to follow the direction of the chief.

3. Keep accurate data using an adequate computer aided dispatch (CAD) and records management system (RMS).

4. Analyze crime occurrences and the deployment of officers to address those issues in real time.

5. Develop a long-term analysis of crime in the iidentified high crime areas and compare the statistics over time for impact of hot-spot policing efforts..

6. And, hold police departments accountable for effective and constitutional policing.

City/area crime rates have always been important for citizens, the media, and people and corporations moving into an area. The Federal Bureau of Investigation (FBI) created the Uniform Crime Reporting system in 1929. Agencies voluntarily report their crime statistics monthly and annually to their state. The state then compiles the data and sends it to the FBI. This makes the comparison of crime rates between cities possible. But not all cities count crime the same way. Police Chiefs have often been accused of pencil whipping crimes to show their police department is having a positive impact. While most of today's Computer Aided Dispatch (CAD) systems automatically compile the data, it takes a police officer to specify what crime was committed when they file their report.

In January 2021, the FBI transitioned from the older Uniform Crime Report (UCR) program to a much more detailed reporting system called the National Incident-Based Reporting System (NIBRS). While more detailed, its expanded list of crime types still depends on an officer's interpretation of what crime occurred. State-wide data from the NIBRS reporting is usually available in some form on state websites. City staff can find and compare this data for both their city and the average for the entire state. Locating your organization's reported NIBRS crime and clearance rates and that of similar jurisdictions or state averages can provide relevant comparisons identifying any crime problems in a given city or district.

Possible Questions for the Police Department

1. Can you provide me with the department's NIBRS report for the end of the last year, and the NIBRS state average for the same period?

2. Does the department have the Computer-Aided Dispatch and Records Management Systems needed for accurate and timely analysis of crime and calls for service?

Chapter 3
Policing – *what does and does not work*

It is easier to start this discussion of what works in policing by listing the things that we know do *not* work. The policing experiments beginning in the 1970s have left a clear trail of strategies that have no apparent impact on crime. We know that when officers randomly drive around the city on preventive patrol trying to cover all areas of the city equally (because all citizens like seeing a police car drive by), does *not* work. It may make a few citizens happier, but it has no demonstrable impact on crime.

Zero-tolerance enforcement was born out of the *Broken Windows* theory first described in 1981. This theory of crime control focused on cleaning up visible crimes such as graffiti, loitering, panhandling and prostitution. While we know that zero-tolerance enforcement of small petty crimes appears to reduce the crime rate, it usually negatively impacts minority groups and increases negative interactions between police and these communities -- reducing public trust. The reduction in crime appears to be temporary, and only while officers are present. These findings make it clear that we cannot arrest our way out of a high crime rate.

Simply adding officers to a department does not reduce crime. Studies have shown that adding officers can actually give the appearance of increased crime because more officers are available to take reports. Remember that not all crime is reported to the police. Serious crimes are reported more often, but even some serious crimes go unreported. The annual National Crime Victimization Study conducted by the Bureau of Justice Statistics shows that only 46 percent of violent victimizations were reported to the police in 2021. More officers can impact crime but they have to be doing the right things. It is more important what they do on patrol and where they do it that the total numbers.

We also know that a fast response to calls for service does not necessarily increase the likelihood of an arrest for most serious crimes. The Kansas City Response Time Experiment found that people often call their friends, husbands, wives, mothers, or fathers first before calling the police. Nevertheless, there are many other reasons to respond quickly to serious calls. These include securing a crime scene to prevent the destruction of evidence, providing medical assistance and identifying witnesses before they leave. Even in less serious crimes, a quick response tells citizens that the police will be there quickly if they really need them.

Many police departments today describe their crime control efforts as "proactive policing." Proactive Policing was first described by Los Angeles Chief William H. Parker in the 1950s. He was one of first to analyze crime patterns, but ordered officers off of walking beats and into cars. Being aggressive and making more arrests, he called this Proactive Policing. In some departments, this means that officers are encouraged to *proactively* engage when they observe suspicious circumstances and take as many active enforcement efforts as possible (arrests or citations) to somehow reduce crime in the process. If this proactive policing is done without proper direction and supervision, it allows officers to make their own decisions about what to do and where to do it. Unrestrained and undirected proactive activity can have a devastating impact on community trust.

We also know that some forms of community policing, like just having a Citizen's Police Academy and volunteer program or having an officer handing out stickers to kids, does not reduce crime. Police agencies must listen to community voices about what they feel is most important. These voices can be from the community itself or through the elected or appointed individuals in the city government. When police respond and address these issues, it increases the trust and legitimacy of the police.

So, what *does* work to reduce crime?

Data-Driven Policing

What appears to work best in today's world is known by several names: data-driven policing, intelligence-led policing, or hot-spot policing. These practices require the use of specific geographic and temporal crime data from the department's dispatch and records management software systems. It requires analyzing where and when the most serious crimes are occurring (identifying hot spots) and intentionally deploying officers in these areas (see **Figure 1**). We know from a multitude of studies that having officers randomly drive around a city to enhance police presence does not affect crime. This is likely because we cannot afford enough officers to make a real threat to offenders of being caught. But we can strategically place officers in smaller areas more often.

Experienced law enforcement professionals do not see most criminals as rational individuals who calculate their risks and rewards before offending. Most criminal activity is both *situational* and *opportunistic*. Very few individuals know the minute they wake up that they are going to do something illegal to get money, but they are a few. It may be cutting off catalytic converters from parked cars or following an elderly person home from a bank and taking their money.

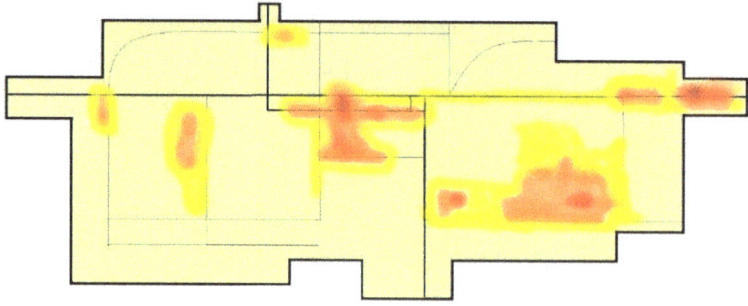

Figure 1: *Crime data from the department's records management system is mapped to show crime hot spots.*

These people, like all humans, are creatures of habit. If it worked yesterday, they expect it will work again today. Knowing where these incidents have occurred allows police to deploy resources to those or similar areas.

Most people arrested have no idea of the Penal Code's definition nor the potential penalty for the crime they have committed. For instance, shoplifting a small item from a store might be considered a petty offense with a small fine. However, if an employee sees a shoplifter and tries to stop them and the shoplifter pushes them down, the crime now becomes a felony robbery with a prison sentence. Randomly patrolling all areas of the city equally does not reduce crime, but intentionally directing officers to conduct specific police engagement activities in smaller hot-spot areas can and does have a significant crime-control effect.

A growing number of recent studies have proved this effect on crime. Several studies even identify the amount of time an officer must spend in the hot spot to create the protective effect. To be effective, these officers need to be seen actively engaging with the community, not just driving through. To be effective, the community and potential offenders need to see the officer walking the area, talking to individuals, making traffic stops, investigating suspicious circumstances, and taking enforcement action. This increases the perception of danger to opportunistic criminals and reduces their likelihood of offending.

The identification of these hot spots within a city must also take into consideration the time element of the offenses. It will do no good to deploy resources to an area in the early morning hours if the crimes are occurring in the late evening.

While the unrestricted use of proactive policing and making large numbers of minor arrests may be problematic if done across an entire city, using these tactics in clearly identified hot-spot areas may be productive. Even then, these activities need to be restricted and closely supervised. Prior to using these tactics, the community should be provided with clear evidence as to why such activities are needed in this limited area and how they will be controlled. Additionally, officers need to be trained specifically in the limitations of their use. Specialized units with no regular call response duties may also be very effective in hot spots, but their operations must be closely controlled and supervised as well to prevent them from conducting inappropriate activities.

Typically, unrestrained proactive policing allows officers to use invasive tactics, such as pretext stops and consent searches anywhere in the city, even in low-crime areas. It allows officers to create their own tactics regardless of legality, they are usually not well-supervised or controlled, and no prior notification of the need for such activities is given to a community. Using proactive efforts in hot spots allows *the department* to establish the defined areas, tactics, approved procedures and level of supervision. Plus, it gives the department an opportunity to involve the community in its plans.

Of course, continuous data analysis is needed to ensure that crime hot spots are not simply displaced to another area. Some criminals commit serial offenses within a city or region, depending on their access to transportation. Constant crime analysis usually identifies these offenses and allows for effective police response. But this requires someone to monitor and analyze the data regularly. This person may be a capable officer or a non-sworn crime analyst with the needed skills. Remarkably, many crime hot spots tend to be in the same place year after year due to the community's physical characteristics and social and economic makeup. In these continuous hot spots with specific crime issues, problem-oriented policing (POP) works best to reduce crime and its impact.

Problem-Oriented Policing

Herman Goldstein first described problem-oriented policing (POP) in 1979. POP identifies a specific crime problem, develops a detailed analysis and its causes, and creates a response with community input and involvement. POP also assesses the response once implemented – thus, reviewing the crime from start to finish. Using POP inside hot spots, where specific environmental factors can be modified to reduce crime opportunities, has had outstanding results.

Police understand that for a crime to occur, several elements are needed. Known as the *crime triangle*, three critical elements are almost always present. They include: a suitable victim; a motivated offender; and an area lacking guardianship or surveillance. When police respond to hot spot crimes, they try to identify the causes of crimes and remove one or more of the contributing factors (see **Figure 2**).

Figure 2: *Illustrated is the crime triangle used in crime prevention analysis. (2023)*

A typical POP project might identify and analyze city locations where the police are most often called or where the same or similar crimes are often committed. Once known, those calls can be reduced by some form of intervention. Analysis of a repeat burglar alarm location may reveal that the employees were not properly trained in how to deactivate the alarm or they may discover a faulty sensor. Examining multiple shoplifting calls made by a big box store might lead to allowing store loss prevention staff to direct file cases to municipal court, without the need for police intervention to respond and issue citations or make arrests.

While POP has been around for decades, few police agencies recognize and use this process. The International Association of Chiefs of Police even created an annual award for the best POP program submitted each year to encourage its use. The "Center for Problem-Oriented Policing," a non-profit organization centered at Arizona State University, provides online access to thousands of successful POP initiatives that have solved crime problems throughout our country. Yet, finding police departments that have trained their officers and actively pursue POP initiatives is still relatively rare.

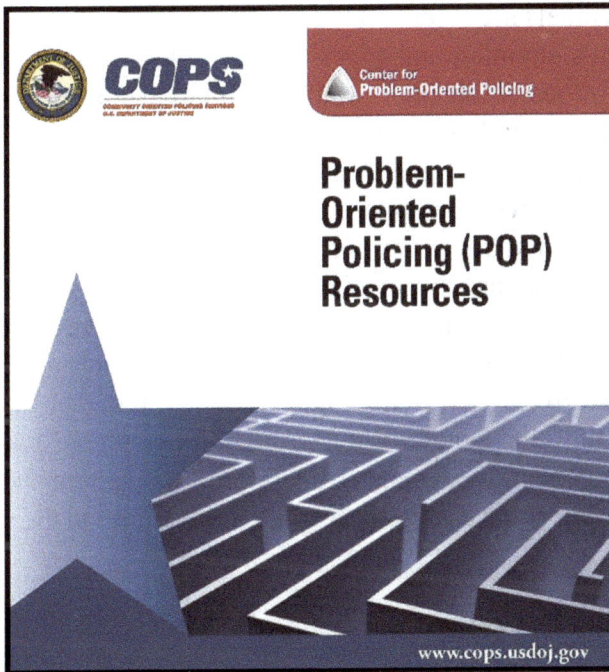

Figure 3: *The Community-Oriented Policing Services (COPS) office has numerous problem-oriented policing resources, US Government. (2011)*

Focused Deterrence

Focused Deterrence can be seen as another form of problem-oriented policing. However, focused deterrence is directed at specific individuals or groups, such as a criminal street gang, committing offenses in a community. Police often identify individuals who are under investigation or they may have developed intelligence indicating that they are involved in criminal activity. Many times, police cannot develop sufficient evidence to prosecute, or cannot prosecute because a victim has been threatened by the perpetrator and declines to prosecute. Obviously, police cannot arrest individuals for what they might do in the future. Nevertheless, there are techniques for influencing individuals' and groups' future activities. For instance, the Boston Ceasefire project was successful at reducing gang-related shootings in South Boston. A group of police, prosecutors and federal judges met with gang leaders and promised federal conspiracy investigations with the intent to arrest gang leaders on any gang-related shootings. Gang leaders would get no plea deals, receive full federal prosecution for all offenses, and no reduction in prison time for good behavior.

Police departments are stretched thin today. Usually, they can't afford the time needed to identify, arrest and prosecute every crime reported. However, if a very few individuals are responsible for a large number of crimes, increasing the department's attention and focus on these individuals can have a significant effect. Increased enforcement strategies include increasing surveillance of individuals, arresting and prosecuting specific individuals for minor crimes, increasing pre-trial sanctions for violent offenses (high or no bond requests), prioritizing warrant service, spending more time developing conspiracy cases, and prosecuting in the federal system, if possible. The federal system does not allow bonds in certain circumstances, fast trials, and serving a higher percentage of the sentence, among others. These initiatives require significant extra work by the police, prosecutors and courts, and are usually used only for the most serious cases. Police have a high degree of enforcement discretion, and using this discretion to the benefit of the community can have a significant effect on crime. Once again, we see the critical need for accurate and timely data to assist in identifying and tracking these groups and individuals.

Community Policing

Community policing is the last big policing initiative, and most departments claim they embrace this model. Just having a Citizen's Academy and handing out stickers to kids is not community policing. Today, community policing consists of training officers to develop relationships within the community, organizing the department to support community policing activities, and creating and using community partnerships in problem-solving activities. This amounts to finding effective ways to listen to community input and involve community members to achieve their desired solutions. Having a citizen's academy is not enough, even though a citizen's academy does produce a better understanding of police in the community and often leads to very active civilian volunteer programs. Community partnerships are easy to set up -- but difficult to nurture and keep active.

Over the years, with the closure or reduction of many social services, the police have been forced into and have accepted roles for which they are not fully qualified. Many community organizations receive grant funding to deal with issues such as homelessness and mental illness. Partnering with these community groups is desperately needed to leverage their expertise and resources to solve these difficult problems.

Problem-oriented policing (POP) often involves developing partnerships for specific crime problems in limited geographic areas. Community policing is slightly different in that it focuses on the entire community. In addition to the Citizen's Academy, you may see patrol officers attending every community event such as monthly PTA meetings, homeowner association meetings and many other gatherings.

Other initiatives might include a Chief's advisory council made up of area residents to discuss policy issues and crime problems; an inter-faith council made up of local pastors to provide input and feedback; citizen feedback systems such as surveys or phone follow-up with police contacts; a significant social media presence with clear feedback mechanisms for commenting on police policy and operations; and regular police supervisor meetings with the Chief where community feedback issues are the main topic. Part of the officer's training would be how to respond and report citizen input (both positive and negative) to the department's command staff. The United States Department of Justice created the Office of Community Policing to provide free training for departments in community policing initiatives and operations.

While there is no clear evidence that agencies highly involved in community policing have significantly lower crime rates, there is clear evidence that these departments generate a greater level of trust and citizen satisfaction. Public trust is critically important in police operations. Individuals in a community will hesitate to get involved, either as a witness to a particular incident or as a participant in collective problem-solving, if they have no trust in their police department.

One of the best examples of a combination of POP and community policing is the Omaha 360 Violence Intervention and Prevention Collaborative. An initiative by Empower Omaha brings together the police department, local churches, organizations and service providers in weekly meetings to discuss recent crimes, what worked the previous week, and what to anticipate for the following week. Each entity then discusses what they could do in an effort to reduce crime in their community. The initiative has been credited with reducing gun violence in Omaha by almost half in recent years.

Looking at a police department from the outside seldom shows the difference between those using these techniques and those who do not. The highest priority for most citizens is for the police to respond quickly when needed. Citizens want assurance that someone can respond to prevent bad things from happening to them. Most police departments do that well. What separates departments is what they do with their time when they are not responding to calls. Of course, this partly depends on whether or not they have the time between calls to do any community crime control.

For any police department to use today's best crime-control techniques, they must have the time to employ these techniques. Also, data analysis to identify a city's problems and high-crime areas is needed. Typically, police officers are not enthusiastic data analysts, but they can learn. Using reliable computer-aided dispatch and records management systems, someone competent in extracting and compiling data is essential for today's efficient and effective policing operation.

Can the police impact crime? Yes, with a combination of data-driven or intelligence-led hot-spot policing, Problem Oriented Policing, focused deterrence strategies, and community policing, police departments have the best chance to reduce serious crime. Cities may still see a reduction in crime, even if their police departments are not doing any of these things. On the other hand, cities can also see a rise in crime even if their department is doing everything right. Overall, crime in our country is controlled by a myriad of forces over which the police have little or no control. But given the massive expense of police agencies, if these agencies are not doing all they can to reduce crime, valuable resources are being wasted.

Possible Questions for the Police Department

1. What specific crime control strategies or tactics do you use to reduce crime?

2. What are the major crime problems in the city and where do they occur?

3. Do you have staff capable of identifying crime hot spots and trends on a regular or continuous basis?

4. What community policing strategies do you use?

5. How do you evaluate your performance in crime control activities?

6. What specific problem-oriented policing (POP) projects has the department implemented this past year, and what are the results?

7. What specific community policing activities and operations does the department currently have in place?

Chapter 4
The Police Organization

The Police Chief

No decision within city government is more critical than the selection of the right person for chief of police. His or her officers carry enormous responsibility. They have the power of the state to deprive a person of their liberty and, in limited circumstances, to use force up to and including deadly force against citizens. Police departments and cities are often sued for negligent hiring, negligent training, negligent supervision, negligent retention, negligent entrustment, failure to train, failure to direct, failure to discipline, and violating an individual's civil rights. Hiring a particular individual as chief because of a powerful group's special interest, or even the person's race, without ensuring that they have the ability to perform, can be disastrous for any city.

When a police chief vacancy occurs, usually one of the first questions asked is should they immediately appoint a lower-ranking department member as the new chief? If the department has been running well with few internal issues and good support in the community, then appointing a chief from within the department may be an easy solution, providing the individual being considered has the desired qualifications. However, if the department has had significant internal personnel issues, problematic community relations, lack of a cohesive vision, or if no one in the department has the desired characteristics, an outside chief may be a better solution. Appointing an officer from inside a troubled department may not correct internal issues as the appointed officer may have been part of the problem.

While a city's Human Resources department may believe they are well qualified to conduct a search for a new police chief, there are significant law enforcement issues for which they have no experience. Cities should be open to requesting assistance from local or state Police Chiefs Associations, or even consulting groups to aid with the selection process. Local area chiefs have a vested interest in making sure a newly selected chief is competent. Most police chiefs' associations can provide competent chiefs from the surrounding area to attend selection boards or interviews to aid in the selection process. If a city decides to go it alone, they are well-advised to first develop the overall goals for the department, then structure candidate interview questions around the candidate's history of achieving those goals and, if selected, how they will go about achieving those goals in their new position. Leveraging what works as discussed in **Chapter 3**, cities will be better prepared to identify good candidates.

There should also be no substitute or short cut to conducting a complete and detailed background investigation on a potential selection, even if coming from inside a department. Funds used to have an outside firm conduct a detailed background investigation can often prevent a serious mistake.

Once hired, police chiefs are immediately immersed in department operations. Because there may have been a period with no chief, there may be many problems that need the chief's immediate attention. This backlog impinges on the new chief's ability to quickly move forward, drowning them in the department's day-to-day activities. In a situation like this, it is up to the city leadership to ensure that the chief does not forget the overall management responsibilities for which they were hired. Ensuring that the chief develops a vision and mission, works with city leadership to create a strategic plan, and reviews and makes necessary policy changes is necessary for cultural change.

Additionally, many people like to believe that once they become chief, they no longer need to receive training. Let us be very clear, no one in the agency is more in need of continuous updated training than the chief. By far, no one else in the organization is more in need of leadership training either. How can you expect an organization to maintain pace with the times if the chief is not aware of the changes? Each city needs to ensure that their chief receives the necessary training to remain current with the latest in policing operations, management skills, and policing philosophy.

Smaller Departments

Most police departments in our country are small, employing less than 25 officers. In these smaller departments officers typically work eight, 10 or even 12-hour shifts. Best practice is to have an assigned supervisor on every shift. This may be a corporal or sergeant, or even just an officer-in-charge because someone needs to be responsible for department operations at all times. Supervisors in smaller departments must wear many hats. The day-shift supervisor may also be responsible for supervising two detectives and managing vehicle fleet maintenance. These small departments simply do not have the resources to have separate individuals doing these tasks, but with smaller departments, these tasks usually do not take much time each day. In addition to managing on-duty personnel, these supervisors may be required to also answer calls and make arrests. When the number of on-duty police personnel reaches four or five officers, the supervisor needs to attend to supervision duties full-time, except when needed as a backup or to supervise a major incident.

Smaller departments are usually organized with a chief, three or four sergeants (one over each of the patrol shifts), and possibly a detective sergeant (over the detectives). Smaller departments usually have about 10-18 percent of their sworn officers as detectives. When departments reach about 10-15 officers, it becomes more effective to have a full-time investigator or detective to conduct follow-up activities on criminal offenses. When departments reach four to five officers on each patrol shift, an additional layer of supervision may be needed. An additional supervisor may be needed to effectively manage a detective unit with four or five detectives, and a dispatch and records function. Chiefs should not have more than four or five direct reports due to their other management responsibilities.

As departments expand, there is a need to coordinate activities between shifts and detectives and dispatch. These operations may become too much for the chief to handle alone. When a department reaches 25-35 sworn officers, it is often more efficient to have a commander over patrol and one over investigations and administration. These commanders can be lieutenants, captains, commanders, or even assistant chiefs, but their salary range should be just above the supervisors they support. Most agencies use lieutenants. An assistant chief is usually unnecessary until an agency reaches the range of 60-75 sworn officers, but some agencies may have significant special needs to warrant one earlier. The best practice is to minimize the levels of supervision as much as possible to keep salary expenses down yet maintain a line supervision ratio of one supervisor for every 6-10 patrol officers, and four to five direct reports for upper-level supervisors and the chief.

Larger Departments

Police departments usually grow with the size and workload of the city. The workload is the citizen's demands for service. Most often this is measured through a department's citizen-generated calls for service. Also growing with a city is the number of various types of crimes requiring specialized responses. As departments grow, it is more efficient to specialize functions. Training is expensive – hence, it is not cost-effective to train all officers in all the specialties needed in larger departments. For instance, a smaller city may experience only a few financial crimes each year with little success in solving them, but as the city grows it may experience more and far greater financial crimes. With proper specialized training, a detective can investigate these crimes, potentially identify the offenders, and prevent future crimes by arrest and prosecution.

Developing specialized functions within a department should be considered carefully as once created, they often take on a life of their own. At that point it is almost impossible to eliminate them, even if the initial justification no longer applies. The investigative unit is usually the largest group of officers outside of patrol. Major cities with over 100 officers will likely have a multitude of specialized officers. Because all police chiefs are aware of the public's desire for the police to respond when they call, chiefs must try to keep patrol staffed -- even when the department is shorthanded. When the department has multiple vacancies, the detectives, community services officers, traffic officers and other personnel often are transferred back to patrol to maintain response capabilities.

Reorganizing departments and reducing specialized positions and supervisors can be very disruptive to a department, especially where officers see these positions as the only way to advance their careers. It is better to carefully consider the initial need for permanent specialized positions or supervisory ranks than to create morale problems by taking them away. In many cases, creating a *task force* to address a particular problem gives the department an opportunity to evaluate the need for a long-term specialized position before creating one.

Police Morale

A very difficult issue for city managers and city councils to address is police morale. Usually, the only time city leaders hear about police morale is when it has hit rock bottom, or officers feel it has never been lower. Police associations, unions, or police groups rarely go before the city council to proclaim, "Morale has never been better!"

Low morale in a police agency, if real and not the creation of a small group who have personal issues, can be detrimental to overall law enforcement operations. Low morale can result in work slowdowns, slow responses, even ineffectual policing. In the years immediately following the George Floyd death in Minneapolis, demonstrations and attempts to defund the police across the country had a devastating effect on police morale. Police officers were vilified, and many responded by barely policing – only doing what was minimally needed. Police officers can easily do only what is required, such as answer calls and make arrests when they have no other choice. Alternatively, they can embrace the directions of their supervisors and commanders and take the initiative to impact crime, such as conducting traffic stops, intervening in threatening situations, and taking proactive efforts to reduce crime in hot spots.

Police departments need assertive, proactive police officers to impact crime. Not aggressive in the physical sense, but aggressive in getting the job done. Bad morale can reduce or eliminate officers' desire to do what the department and city wants done. Because officers work independently, they must have the personal drive to investigate a suspicious incident or initiate a traffic stop when they see a violation. Without that personal initiative, they will just answer calls and pretend not to see the suspicious circumstance that may lead to a crime, or not see the traffic violation that may later result in a fatal accident. When officers feel undervalued and unsupported, they have little job satisfaction and little self-initiative. Hence, service delivery declines. To keep morale up, managers and councils should make every effort possible to show officers their appreciation for the job they do and recognize outstanding performance.

Often poor morale results from internal issues. When these issues develop, employee groups may circulate a survey (whether formal or informal) within a department to gauge morale or the confidence officers have in a chief. These surveys are often designed by police associations with the clear intent to prove that morale is low. While some management practices can cause low morale, it is important to determine the true causes and extent of an issue once it surfaces. Indeed, in some cases poor morale can develop simply from a police chief doing exactly what needs to be done and what a manager or council should support.

Generally, police departments are not democracies. As such, the officers should not run the department. While officers, even those with very little experience, can develop very efficient ways of handling problems, they often do not have the experience to evaluate whether their methods are acceptable or reasonable within the community they serve. The reason the state requires police officers to be hired by a governmental unit and not work independently is to allow proper oversight of their activities. Cities hire police chiefs to ensure that their departments are run appropriately. Unfortunately, like doctors, lawyers, and even city managers, some police chiefs are not always as good or as competent as they should be. Being human, each has their own set of strengths and weaknesses. Holding officers accountable for complying with directives and doing the job in the manner prescribed, instead of the way they may want to do it or the way they have always done it, can sometimes be a catalyst for bad morale.

Before developing solutions to a bad morale problem, it is critical to determine the cause and extent of the problem. Using an outside consultant without a preconceived agenda may be the best option in these cases. Neutral employee surveys, interviews, and focus groups (where anonymity can be guaranteed) can identify any contributing factors and determine the extent of the problem.

Police associations exist to benefit their *members*. Police departments exist to benefit *communities*. Both are important, but sometimes their goals can conflict. Regardless of any conflict between these two groups, police leadership must try to accomplish both at the same time. This requires the chief to be open and honest with all employees. The chief needs to establish constant communication and meetings and both commend and discipline officers, depending on the circumstance. Plus, it takes time. It also requires employee engagement at a level not seen in prior decades.

Today's generation of police officers demand that they be a part of the process. To do this takes a lot of work – but it can be done. In some cases, if the situation has gone on too long and personal grudges have developed between the officers and a chief, the only solution may require a change in personnel. Fortunately, many times these issues can be managed without such drastic actions, providing that the chief is willing and able to put in the work and be open to ideas and suggestions that do not interfere with the overall goal of the department. Above all else in today's police department, a chief must be a communicator, engaging employees at every opportunity, and creating opportunities for communication where none currently exist.

Possible Questions for the Police Department

1. In the department, what is the current relationship between the officer's association and management?

2. Does the officer's association impact the chief's decision on discipline?

3. Do all department managers and supervisors support the department's vision statement?

4. What are the most significant officer concerns in the department?

Chapter 5
Strategic Planning

One of the easiest ways to tell if a department is trying to impact crime is to look at the department's strategic plan. These plans identify the goals the organization is trying to achieve. Strategic plans are developed by police departments and cities to cover three to five years into the future and should be updated annually at a minimum. These plans should represent both what the police department understands they need to be doing, as well as what the council and citizens believe the police should be doing. If the police department's plans are just in the mind of the police chief, and they are not clearly communicated to the entire department, there should be no surprise when the department doesn't meet its goals.

A strategic plan makes the desired future happen instead of just letting anything happen. It establishes direction and focuses departmental efforts to achieve clearly stated goals. Not every future situation can be anticipated. However, when an issue does arise, the department's strategic plan can help those in charge make decisions regarding that issue. Strategic plans also identify who in the organization is responsible for achieving specific goals.

There are many possible designs for strategic plans. A good strategic plan identifies the department's ultimate goals, and the steps needed to achieve these goals. This includes who is responsible for accomplishing each of the steps, and the timeframe for the actions. For a chief to develop an effective strategic plan, it begins by having discussions with citizens through meetings or surveys, and with the council and city administration. Input from all levels of the police organization is also important as they have a unique perspective on the safety of a city. These discussions should focus on what the city wants in the future, and the methods and means it will use to get there. Developing the main goals relevant for effective police operations allows the police department to evaluate its present resources, plan out budget requests needed to accomplish the goals, and develop periodic objectives (usually annually) to measure progress toward goals. The final strategic plan needs to be reviewed and approved by both the city administration and council to ensure all goals are consistent with the intentions of city leadership.

Once approved, the police chief must ensure that the full plan, as well as the individual shorter-term objectives, are clearly communicated to all members of the department. Internal strategies can then be developed to accomplish the department's approved objectives, operations and policies. Strategic plan objectives can even be pushed down into individual employee performance goals so that each employee's goals mesh with the overall department strategy. The department's objectives must be clear, achievable, and measurable.

No issues are off limits when it comes to planning strategic goals. Potential strategic plan goals include crime control measures, traffic management, community engagement and building community trust, internal support (including equipment, facilities, and training), improving diversity, and ensuring unbiased policing. In some cities these strategic plans have been incorporated into the budget request documents as performance measures. This approach ensures that the council or board has the opportunity and responsibility to review these items each year.

Strategic plans are one of the best methods for accomplishing goals. Because they function much like a report card, they force departments to make every effort to accomplish their goals. Periodic reporting to management and council (discussed in more detail in **Chapter 7**) should include progress towards the objectives identified in the strategic plan. Strategic plans do not have a prescribed format, but many examples can be found by looking online at what other police agencies are doing. Some police chief associations have guides for preparing plans with a multitude of online resources for developing a strategic plan. Agencies without a formal written strategic plan are often those that have little direction, control or accountability.

Possible Questions for the Police Department

1. Can you provide me with the police department's strategic plan?

2. How and when was this plan developed, and when was it last updated?

3. Who was involved in the development of the plan?

4. What current constraints prevent you from accomplishing these goals?

Chapter 6
Police Staffing Levels

Police Operations

Cities have struggled to determine how many police officers are needed ever since police departments were first formed. There are no laws or rules requiring cities to staff a police department at a certain level. Police staffing is optional and most likely becomes a local financial and political decision. Whatever staffing level is provided, the police usually self-adjust in order to perform the most needed and necessary services. Staffing decisions are based on what the city can afford and the level of services they want. It is the police chief's job to utilize the resources he or she is given in the best manner possible.

Police departments are self-adjusting. This means that they will always do the most important things first. If a dispatcher receives a call about a stolen bike from school, while at the same time receives a domestic violence call -- the officers will always take the more important or critical call first. Over time however, the lack of proper staffing will diminish the department's ability to conduct crime control activities and reduce even the most basic response services. Some larger cities can address this issue by reducing a variety of services – such as not responding or investigating minor motor vehicle accidents, not sending officers to certain types of theft calls, and perhaps not sending officers to residential burglaries unless they are in progress.

Moreover, cities cannot afford to staff police departments to a level where they can handle every worst-case scenario. At best, cities will staff agencies to a level where they can handle the average number of service calls expected and have sufficient time available to conduct a minimum of officer-initiated crime prevention or crime control activities. Many cities cannot do even this, but departments must simply do the best they can. All but the very largest cities must rely on mutual aid from other departments, the sheriff's office, or state police in times of critical incidents.

Police chiefs can get the impression that their agency is understaffed when officers complain about running from call-to-call, when dispatchers or citizens report long response times, or when citizens complain that their case is not being followed up. In some cases, chiefs or councils decide they want to expand services and add a specific unit or operation. How do you show a need to a budget-strapped city manager or council? How does a council determine if a request is reasonable?

When chiefs, city managers, or councils believe there is a need for additional officers, there needs to be some way to identify what an appropriate staffing level should be. This staffing will depend on what type of police department the community wants. If they want a bare-bones police department that just answers emergency calls for help and drives around when not busy, you will not need as many officers. However, if they want a progressive department that works to intercept and prevent crime, solve neighborhood quality of life problems, improve community trust, and provide for a safe and secure city, hiring more officers may be the best or only option.

Historically, professional police organizations recommended a certain number of officers per 1,000 population, usually three officers per thousand residents. Another formula used in the past was to use 1/3 of an officer's time on call, 1/3 of their time on patrol, and 1/3 of their time on administrative duties. Neither of these methods took into consideration the community differences and the desires of each community. At about the same time as many of the research studies were being conducted in the 1970s, the Rand Corporation developed the Patrol Car Allocation Model.

This was the first computer-assisted model that computes the time needed to answer calls, the time needed to patrol every city street every so many hours, as well as the necessary administrative time. These times are then combined to determine the number of officers needed. The model takes a significant amount of data collection which usually requires a consultant with experience using the model. Policing research conducted and published after the model was developed tends to downplay the need to patrol all parts of the city and that adding officers to accomplish this may not be productive. Some consultants still use a modified version of this program to develop patrol staffing levels.

The method of determining appropriate patrol staffing now recommended by both the International City Managers Association and the International Association of Chiefs of Police is the time required or workload model. There are several versions of this model, but all divide a police officer's daily activities into three parts: 1) administrative time; 2) service calls; and 3) uncommitted time.

Administrative time accounts for the unrecoverable time away from actual police work that is either granted to officers as part of their employment contract or by law or is the result of their law enforcement activities. This time includes holidays, vacation, sick time, bereavement leave, military leave, and other paid leave granted by a city. It also includes the administrative time that an officer spends each working day to include shift briefing, in-service training, lunch and other breaks, court, vehicle maintenance, and the like. The time used in these administrative activities can be computed by reviewing reports from the Personnel or Finance department's printout of employee time records.

The administrative time on each working shift can be closely estimated by the department's command staff. Each officer is usually paid for 80 hours every two weeks or a total of 2080 hours in a year. The average administrative or unrecoverable time is then subtracted from this, leaving the average number of hours an officer will spend doing police work that year. Most departments range from about 1350 to 1450 hours available per officer for actual productive work hours in a year after administrative time is removed. After the administrative time is removed, the rest of an officer's time is spent either responding to calls for service or conducting proactive policing duties (we hope). Poor direction and poor supervision can result in some less motivated officers just driving around waiting on the next call.

Service calls take into consideration the total number of hours required to respond to and handle the average number of citizens' calls for service. It can be determined very accurately by using the past year's number of citizen-generated calls for service multiplied by the average time on call, resulting in a total number of *officer hours* needed to answer these calls. This data is captured by the department's CAD system along with the data needed to compute average response times.

The workload model has an advantage in that the department or city can use this data to determine more precisely the current percentage of uncommitted time, or to select whatever percentage of uncommitted time they desire in order to determine the number of officers needed to reach that level.

Uncommitted time is the time that officers have to conduct self-initiated activities such as traffic stops, investigating suspicious activities, spending time in identified hot-spots, or working on problem-oriented problems. Studies of various departments have determined that departments with less than 40 percent uncommitted time (time not responding to citizen's calls for service) have great difficulty in conducting meaningful community policing activity and problem-solving. If there is less than 40 percent uncommitted time, that time is usually broken up into such small increments in between calls that they are not productive. (For example, an officer wants to work on a neighborhood drug problem in area A, but is dispatched to a call in area B. As soon as he clears the call, he heads back to Area A. However, after he arrives and sets up surveillance, he gets another call to go back to area B.) This doesn't mean it can't be done as innovative management techniques can free up some blocks of time, providing the citizen call load will allow. Most agencies today that want to conduct community policing (partnerships with the community and neighborhood for problem-solving) attempt to staff their department with at least 40 to

45 percent uncommitted time in patrol.

Knowing the total number of hours needed for answering citizens' calls for service and the desired percentage of uncommitted time desired allows you to compute the total policing hours needed. You next divide the total policing hours needed by the average number of hours available per officer to produce the number of officers needed in patrol.

Appendix A provides the basic method of determining a department's current uncommitted time. If less than 40 percent, your agency will have difficulty in impacting crime in a meaningful way. **Appendix B** provides the basic method of determining the number of patrol call-answering personnel needed after inputting the desired uncommitted time percentage. The more accurate the data obtained and identified, the more accurate the results. For instance, the CAD system may only be able to give the average time on call for all officers responding to all calls for service. However, if the system can separate the average time on call for each officer assigned to calls (some calls require two or more officers depending on the nature of the call – and the second officer usually spends less time on a call), and the number of these two and three officer calls, then the actual data will be more accurate.

This staffing model does not work well when the department size is less than 10-15 officers or fewer than two or three officers per patrol shift. While you can still run the data to see the outcomes, these departments often have more concerns about minimum staffing and officer safety than uncommitted time. Cities still make better decisions by having the most data available.

Shift Scheduling

It is also wise to review the shift schedule periodically. Police departments work a variety of shifts, with 8, 10, and 12-hour shifts being the most popular. Many agencies have gone to the 12-hour shifts because officers enjoy having a three-day weekend every other weekend. Other cities have gone to 12-hour shifts because their surrounding cities have gone to that shift schedule and are more attractive to new recruits than those working 8 or 10-hour shifts.

Shift schedules need to be arranged in a manner that has officers available to answer the calls from citizens when they come in. Most departments' CAD systems can produce data on the total number of calls received by the hour of the day and day-of-week for any time period. Dividing those numbers by the number of days in the time period will provide the average number of calls by the hour of day. This pattern of calls for service is remarkably similar between cities (see **Table 1**).

Table 1: *This table shows the average number of calls for service from citizens by hour of day. It helps to determine the best shift assignment to cover calls with available staff. (2023*

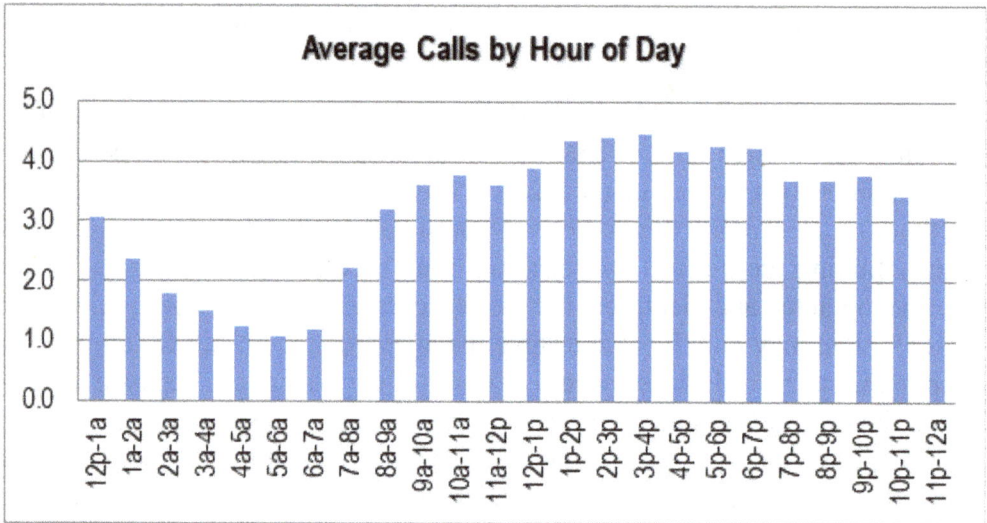

Average Calls by Hour of Day

This pattern is similar for all cities regardless of the total number of calls. Early morning hours are always very low while afternoon and early evening hours are always high. The only difference is with cities where there are large numbers of bars and restaurants that serve alcohol and stay open late. In these cities, the call load usually begins dropping in the early evening and then rises again beginning about 11 pm and staying high until about 2 am.

Producing this data for your city and matching it with the current staffing levels for each hour of the day can identify times when staffing is short and where staffing needs to be improved. **Table 2** shows the calls and officers by hour of day with the same number of officers working each shift. There is no rule that all officers must work the same number of hours or the same shifts each day. For instance, some cities have officers on 12-hour shifts, but some older officers dislike the 12-hour shift. Hence, these officers might be scheduled to work 8-hour shifts during the highest call load period. Most 12-hour shifts change shifts at either 6 am and 6 pm, or 7 am and 7 pm.

Table 2: *Average calls for service with officers assigned by hour of day. This chart shows the average of seven officers assigned on each of two twelve-hour shifts. Note the excess of officers during the early morning hours and the potential shortage of officers in the early afternoon. (2023)*

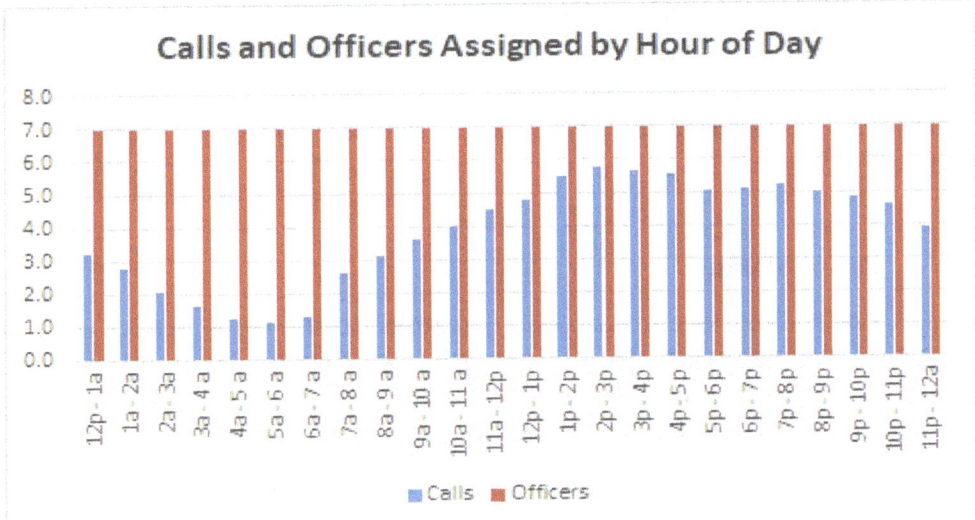

Calls and Officers Assigned by Hour of Day

To better cover the call load, some 12-hour night shifts might have some officers come in at 12 pm to assist in covering the high call load, then go home at 12 am when the need has dropped significantly. **Table 3** shows the same call load with two of the seven (12-hour) night shift officers coming in at noon and working until midnight.

Table 3: *Average calls for service with officers assigned by hour of day. This chart shows staffing with two night-shift officers, both working from noon to midnight. Note the better fit for covering calls for service in the after-noon and lower staffing in the early morning hours. (2023)*

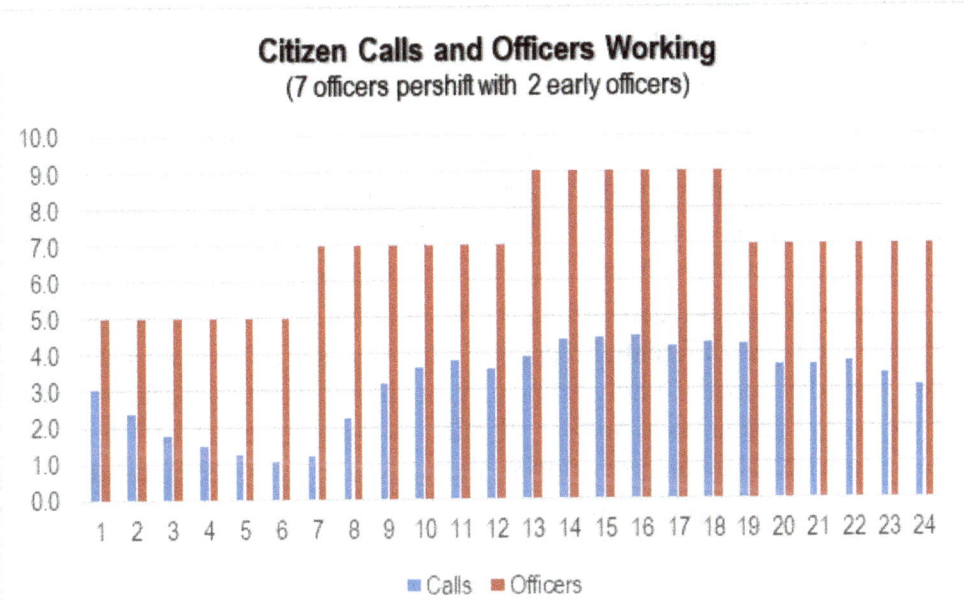

Citizen Calls and Officers Working
(7 officers pershift with 2 early officers)

By fitting officers into the call load, these officers will have a much better response time and a more equal workload. Obtaining this data from the CAD system and allowing officers input into the shift patterns, while making sure that the officers are present for the workload, can have a positive effect on officer morale and improve operations.

Patrol Staffing

The staffing level of a police department can have a number of consequences that may not be immediately apparent. In very small departments, it may mean that there are few and, in some cases, only a single officer on a shift. Many small departments must rely on mutual aid from the Sheriff's Department, the State Police, or other local law enforcement officers. However, when these resources are unavailable, officers may have to answer very dangerous calls alone.

We know from the Kansas City Preventive Patrol Experiment that randomly driving around the area to prevent crime has no impact on crime or citizen perceptions of crime. This experiment, done in 1973, compared patrol beats in Kansas City using a host of critical measures before and after the test. The study compared the following three scenarios: 1) five beats with no preventative patrols; 2) five beats with double the preventative patrols; and 3) five beats with the standard number of preventative patrols. After detailed evaluations, they found no significant difference in the outcome measures. But we now know clearly that if the patrol officers have the available time, spending as little as 15 minutes every two hours in a crime hot spot, engaging in some form of police activity can reduce crime. Insufficient officers to allow for this engagement time during a shift can completely reduce the department's ability to impact crime. Agencies with very low uncommitted time (time not answering calls) will see traffic stops decline, self-initiated activity and arrests decline, and officers will just be responding to calls and taking reports. Reduced staffing will also force officers to "hurry up" on calls because they know another call may be holding. Reducing this time available to officers reduces their ability to use the recommended procedural justice techniques of letting people tell their story,

Police agencies faced staffing shortages in the 1970s and 1980s developed what is known as differential response. This is when formal call priority systems were developed. Clearly, some calls are more urgent than others. Because of the lack of resources to answer all calls immediately, cities had to prioritize their response. They also developed alternatives to patrol response for many lower priority calls, such as telephone reporting and now online police reports where citizens can report crimes online. If smaller agencies are not using these alternative measures to reduce patrol workload, they should be encouraged to do so. A one-time expenditure for software or programming may be far less expensive than increasing patrol staffing permanently.

Another result of not having enough patrol officers is an increase in response times to calls for service. Response time – the time it takes an officer to get to the scene once dispatched – is a function of availability, distance, and speed. Response speeds are fairly consistent based on the street and highway geography. Typically, officers are only allowed to exceed the speed limit when running with lights and sirens, and most police agencies limit those responses to emergencies, or priority one calls only. With fewer officers on duty, or if on-duty officers are tied up on a call, the average distance other officers must travel to respond to a call increases. As such, the time it takes to get there increases as well. If no officers are available or are on a call, the citizen may have to wait for a police response, sometimes with horrible results.

Typically, police chiefs are aware of these issues and make every attempt to keep patrol as full as possible given their staffing limitations. Often this means that the chief will move officers from more specialized jobs in the department back into patrol to keep response times low, and to ensure officer safety. This means that many of the specialized functions such as the Community Relations officer, Criminal Investigation Division (CID) detectives, and traffic officers are moved back into patrol. Thus, the department's performance in these areas will begin to suffer. Citizens will see a decrease in community activities, crime clearance rates will drop, and traffic tickets issued will decline. (Specialized traffic enforcement officers routinely do not answer calls and spend their entire shifts on traffic enforcement activities. These officers usually issue significantly more citations daily than patrol officers.)

Not having enough officers in patrol and moving officers from other specialized jobs in the department can also have a negative effect on morale. Officers who worked for years to obtain these coveted jobs are now forced back into patrol. It also results in not being able to grant officers accrued time off for holidays, vacation and compensatory time. While most officers abide by these decisions, after being denied a particular day off, some will call in sick to take the day off anyway. Officers may not be able to attend family events and as a result, officer morale suffers.

With fewer officers to handle the load, department overtime will also likely increase. Officers usually try to complete their necessary reports before clearing a call and going on to the next. Inappropriately staffed departments force officers to routinely go from call to call, delaying their report writing time for later. With high call load in the late afternoons, time often runs out at the end of the shift and officers must use overtime to complete their reports. While supervisors can relieve some of this time stress by telling officers they can do their reports the next day, critical reports must still be done for investigations to continue and to capture details while they are still fresh in the officer's mind. Plus, there will be a whole new batch of calls coming in during the next shift. This all causes late relief overtime to rise.

Understandably, many bad things can happen when agencies are inappropriately staffed. But what if your tax base is not keeping up with your city's needs? For example, what if your fire department needs a new engine, and two of your three garbage trucks just broke? Often in situations like this, city managers and councils will just have to make tough decisions. Some cities can only afford a bare-bones police department, so they have to be satisfied with that. When this happens, these decisions must be clearly communicated to the officers and employees to at least let them know the why behind the decisions. It is up to the police chief to do the best job possible with what they have.

When financial times are tight there are some less expensive options and some alternatives for reducing the call load for patrol. Non-sworn or civilian staff can do many things in a police department that do not require a badge and gun. Officers are paid higher because they carry the responsibility of deciding when to take away someone's liberty, or when it is necessary to use deadly force. Civilians or non-sworn staff can answer many of the non-dangerous calls for service such as a report of vehicle burglary, or a shoplifting report where the offender has left the scene.

The Los Angeles Police Department now operates a system where non-sworn staff respond to 29 different types of service calls where armed officers previously had to respond. Civilians can do a great deal of routine investigative work in CID and even community services. Conveniently, civilians are usually paid less and are easier and faster to hire. While they still must undergo a background investigation before having access to criminal histories and state databases, the process is usually much quicker. Care must be exercised however when certain assigning calls to unarmed civilians because it is possible that citizens may fail to communicate the potential danger of a call, potentially putting the responding civilian staff at risk.

Cities also can add crime reporting options by training current civilian staff to take telephone reports, or even implement online reporting. When dispatchers receive a call where someone is requesting a report, they can be directed to the other options rather than always sending a patrol officer.

Criminal Investigations Staffing

The Criminal Investigations Division (CID) is generally the second largest unit within a police department, although sometimes it can consist of one officer. When patrol has arrested a suspect, most often CID will put the case package together and do follow-up tasks – such as getting medical records and doing detailed interviews before filing the case with the county or state attorney's office. If the patrol officer did not make an arrest at the scene or shortly thereafter, CID is usually responsible for doing the follow-up investigation in an attempt to identify, locate, and arrest an offender.

Properly staffing an investigative unit is not as straightforward as staffing patrol. This is because there is no standard for time spent on a burglary investigation or a robbery investigation. Every case is different. And there is no guarantee that if you spend a standard amount of time on a case, or even twice or three times the average amount of time on a case, you will be successful at identifying the offender. Some cases simply cannot be solved with the information police are able to develop. Different operational policies, such as assigning every case to a detective or using an effective case screening system can also impact the time available. The detective can always do more investigation, but with no guarantee of any results.

Numerous studies have concluded that detectives or investigators actually solve very few crimes; however, citizens still expect the department to try. Almost 90 percent of all arrests are made by patrol (with some of those being on warrants initiated by detectives). All research indicates that if you want to increase the number of case clearances, the best way is to improve the patrol officer's preliminary investigation. But detectives do solve some crimes. And most of the time these are the high-profile, violent crimes, like murder, rape, and robbery, that impact a citizen's fear of crime.

Annual national victimization studies done by the Department of Justice (DOJ) indicate that less than half of all crime is reported to the police. A "Clearance" is when a responsible party (a suspect) is arrested, or where the department has identified the offender and his location but is unable to proceed with prosecution due to such factors as the victim being unwilling to prosecute. Police agencies seldom clear over 30 percent of crimes reported to them with patrol responsible for most of the arrests. Smaller cities usually clear a higher percentage than larger agencies.

So, what should the goal be for a criminal investigation unit? Clearing more than the state average number of cases for similar size cities is a good start. And how many detectives do you need to do that?

Detectives or investigators also have administrative time that cannot be used for police work. They also receive holidays and vacation time. Usually more senior officers will have more vacation and sick time. They also have administrative activities every day they are at work. They have lunch, breaks, attend court more often, and frequently have other duties such as being a court bailiff. Studies conducted in many departments show that detectives have slightly fewer hours available for actual police investigative work than patrol officers – usually around 1,300 to 1,400 total hours per year.

In the early 1980s, agencies in Florida began developing a standard detective staffing model. Different department planning and research officers asked detectives to keep track of their time spent on various types of investigations for months at a time. The initial results were quite crude, but refinements over time developed a model that most major consulting companies use today as national benchmarks. In tests using more sophisticated time required models, these national benchmarks produce the same or very similar results. The workload models require significantly more detailed input, which must be obtained by having the detectives track the time spent on different types of cases over several months. While this may better reflect the investigative style of one particular agency, it is seldom worth the time and detective complaints when the national benchmarks appear to work just as well.

These national benchmarks are separated into three basic categories and are intended for agencies that investigate crimes against persons and crimes against property. Generally, this is the first level of specialization that most agencies use. The next level of specialization is usually some form of financial crimes. Applying these benchmarks is relatively simple given the number of cases assigned to detectives over time.

National Benchmarks

Crimes Against Persons:	8 – 12 new cases per month
Crimes Against Property:	15 – 20 new cases per month
Financial Crimes:	10 – 20 new cases per month

Since crimes against persons usually only amounts to about 10 percent of all cases, agencies that do not specialize should use a 10-18 cases per month benchmark for all cases assigned. Agencies that staff their investigative units to this level are usually able to clear the average or better than the average number of cases. Agencies that have this staffing and are not able to clear an average number of cases will likely have other issues, such as ineffective case screening or other duties that take detectives away from working cases. Larger agencies with more than 40-50 detectives should use more sophisticated workload models because of the significant costs involved in adding or underutilizing detectives.

These benchmarks are intended to be used by agencies with a good case screening system in place. *Case screening* means only assigning cases that are important enough to investigate and only those with workable leads for an investigator to follow. This decision is most often made by a detective supervisor who reviews and assigns all cases in the unit. Even though citizens expect every case to be investigated fully, many cases are simply not worth the time and effort of a detective. Cases like homicides and sexual assaults will always be assigned, but some minor theft cases may depend on the number of available detectives. Both individual detectives and entire investigative units must prioritize their work to produce the greatest benefit. When agencies experience a staffing shortage, detectives are frequently moved from CID back to patrol, and the investigative unit must adjust to assigning fewer cases for follow-up.

Just as in patrol, however, there are ways to better manage the investigations unit workload. The first is effective case screening. It makes no sense to assign a case to a detective when it has no workable leads (excluding serious persons crimes.) When a detective receives a case with no workable leads, he or she must spend time reviewing the case and depending on department policy, must call the victim and often play telephone tag. This takes valuable time away from cases that could be solved.

The Police Executive Research Foundation, in one of its earlier research projects involving police investigations, recommended classifying cases into three tiers: 1) cases where the suspect is in custody (where the case must be prepared for filing); 2) cases where the case could be solved with a reasonable amount of investigation; and 3) cases that would likely not be solved with a reasonable amount of investigation. Classifying cases in this manner takes the eye of an experienced detective or supervisor reading each case before deciding whether or not to assign the case. Assigning only those where the suspect is in custody (to improve the case before filing), or those with a chance of solution frees the detective from many unproductive cases.

Another method of sparing more time for investigators to spend on their cases that might be solved is by removing the extra duties that many departments place on detectives. Many departments have detectives conducting crime scene evidence collection and preservation duties, conducting firearms training, pulling digital evidence from cell phones and vehicle systems, managing the property and evidence facility, running vehicles to the shop for maintenance, and working as court bailiffs. These duties take time away from investigations and could be done much more efficiently by a civilian or non-sworn employee. Again, civilians can be used for many routine duties in an investigation unit – and at a much lower cost and usually with higher efficiency.

Traffic Unit Staffing

Cities with significant highway miles within their jurisdiction often designate separate traffic enforcement officers when the department reaches 40 to 50 officers. As the city and department grow, this function may become a standalone unit with separate supervisors and separate goals from patrol. In most cities a common complaint is speeding in residential neighborhoods. While patrol officers can and do make traffic stops, they must always answer citizens' calls first and see traffic stops as an if you have time task. Officers with primary traffic enforcement duties see their job as traffic enforcement first and backing up patrol and calls for service second.

Vehicle accidents kill and injure almost three times the number of people than criminal activity. Numerous studies show that traffic enforcement can and does save lives and property. Some cities rely on municipal court revenue for necessary city operations, but the cities run the risk of damaging their police department's reputation and trust in the community if they press the department for more revenue. Traffic enforcement should be about reducing deaths and injuries caused by vehicle accidents, not about generating revenue.

In the 1960s and 1970s, police researchers developed what is known as the Traffic Enforcement Index – or the number of convictions for hazardous traffic violations needed to impact or reduce injury traffic accidents. While the research clearly advised that each city should develop its own index based on its own data, many cities simply did not have the long-term data necessary to compute their own index. A few cities have found that around 20 citations per injury or fatality accident were sufficient to change driving behavior enough to reduce accidents. Cities began using the number of 20 to 30 hazardous citations per injury accident as their goal. Using this index, a city with an average of 50 injury accidents a year should attempt to issue a minimum of 1,000 hazardous citations a year to reduce accidents. Issuing regulatory and equipment violations did not seem to have an impact on accidents. While using this index has diminished over the years, additional activities such as traffic enforcement cameras, driving under the influence (DUI) checkpoints, and high-visibility targeted enforcement efforts have gained in popularity.

Assigning officers to traffic enforcement duties alone (with the understanding that they will support patrol when needed) without specific direction and supervision is less effective. Once again, allowing individual officers to decide when and where they make traffic stops and what violations they enforce is less effective than data-driven instructions and supervision. One of the best practices for traffic enforcement is to periodically analyze when and where accidents are occurring in the city, and which violations are causing those accidents. Directing enforcement at these locations when accidents occur, and for the violation identified can significantly reduce crashes. Surprisingly, some studies show that both crime hot spots and vehicle crash locations are often the same. In these cases, traffic officers conducting enforcement in the hot spot/high-crash location can have double the impact.

Traffic officers usually receive special training in accident reconstruction.

They are then given the responsibility to investigate all accidents when the officer is on duty, as well as being called out to serious crashes, if needed. Holding at-fault drivers accountable for serious injuries and deaths from crashes requires detailed technological investigations of the causes.

Citations are not issued at every traffic stop. Many times, officers use their discretionary authority to simply warn the individual. The percentage of citations to traffic stops varies by agency, usually ranging from 40 to 75 percent of stops resulting in a citation. Most states prohibit a quota for citations, but not traffic stops. Although a citation has a greater impact on the actual driver than a warning, traffic stops are still effective -- even without a citation being issued. Citizens who see traffic stops are dissuaded from traffic violations and potential criminals are dissuaded from activity in that area. Once again, when patrol staffing drops, traffic officers are one of the first to be pulled back into patrol. This happens because they are already uniformed and used to working both traffic and patrol calls. The shortage in patrol, when traffic officers are reassigned, usually results in a reduced number of traffic stops and citations.

The impact of conducting traffic stops cannot be understated. Traffic stops are one of the primary methods of intercepting criminal activity in a community. Timothy McVey, the Oklahoma City bomber was caught on a traffic stop by an alert Oklahoma State Trooper. Officers who observe a traffic violation have the authority to stop and identify the driver and issue a citation or summons. This also allows the officer to observe and investigate the vehicle for possible involvement in criminal activity. For instance, observing the interior of the vehicle and its contents or even questioning the driver can lead to further investigation and discovery of another crime.

Oftentimes officers have detailed descriptions of vehicles used in serious criminal offenses and may observe a similar vehicle being driven. Depending on the circumstances, the officer may have sufficient probable cause to make a traffic stop, such as knowing the identity of the driver and the existence of a warrant for the driver. If independent probable cause is not present, the Supreme Court allows officers to stop the vehicle, identify the driver, and investigate further, providing the officer observes an actual traffic code or other criminal violation (pre-text stops.) Lately these pre-text stops have come under increased scrutiny. Some cities have considered prohibiting stopping vehicles for non-hazardous violations, but traffic stops are still one of the most effective methods of identifying individuals involved in criminal activity.

Traffic stops can be abused by officers, so department supervisors need to constantly watch for anomalies in traffic stop videos, citations, and citizen complaints. But traffic stops are effective both in reducing traffic accidents *and* reducing criminal activity. Traffic stops resulting in citations or summons greatly reduce repeated violations by the driver and passengers of a vehicle; have an impact on other drivers who see the traffic stop by dissuading them from traffic violations; and dissuade potential criminals from committing violations near the area -- at least for the next few hours. Traffic stops resulting in warnings have a somewhat lesser effect on the driving behavior of the driver. However, it still can have a positive effect on the driver and passenger's opinion of the officer and department because a warning was issued versus a citation. A stop resulting in only a warning continues to have the same effect on other drivers and potential criminals who observe the stop.

Staffing a traffic officer or unit has no specific formula or process as each city's geography and needs are different. Much like the ancillary duty positions described below, the police chief, city manager, and council need to clearly see the need for traffic officers and have reliable data on which to make their staffing decisions. Primary data needed for these decisions include the number, locations, time of day, and causes of accidents in the city. Any approved position should be staffed to the hours and days of the week when most accidents are occurring. Over time, some of these specialized units tend to migrate to the day shift with Saturday and Sunday off when they are actually needed on other days and times. This again can harm the patrol officer's morale when they have to work the accidents or offenses that they believe should have been worked by specialized unit officers.

Ancillary Sworn Officer Positions

There is a myriad of specialized functions within a police agency where services are performed for the benefit of the citizens. In smaller departments, officers may be tasked with several functions, but as departments grow it becomes more efficient to have a specialized officer perform the function. In some departments, officers have moved into these positions because they no longer want to work patrol, or because they did something, and the chief cannot let them continue to work the street. In most cases, officers move to these positions because they have the desire to specialize in that area of law enforcement and enjoy doing the work. Most are extremely productive in their work. Even so, supervision is still necessary.

Specialized units include:

Community Services	Commercial vehicle enforcement
Fugitive Unit	Narcotics
Vice enforcement	K-9
DWI enforcement	School resource officers
Special events	Victim Services

Gang unit   Homeless outreach
Tourism Unit   Police Recruiter
Court bailiffs   Specialized deployment units
Full-time SWAT

There are no staffing models or even suggestions on when or if these units are needed. They are specific to the needs of a city. Often, they develop because the city leadership identifies a need. Next the city manager and chief conduct an analysis to determine whether or not the services required can be accomplished by the current staff. In other circumstances, the chief may identify a need from internal data analysis and recommend additions to staff that are then considered and approved by the governing body.

Of late, specialized crime impact units have also come under increased scrutiny. These units have always been a "go to" tool for police departments and some chiefs to show citizens they are getting tough on crime. These specialized units, when properly directed and properly supervised, can have a significant effect on crime hot spots and can seriously reduce crime. Unfortunately, many of these units are not properly directed or supervised. Some officers believe that since they are a *"special unit"* that they somehow have a license to do things differently than what is usually acceptable.

This attitude has led some units to abuse citizens, increase use of force (pushing and even exceeding legal limits), and the use questionable tactics and arrests. A critical aspect of creating units of this nature, which can be very effective in carefully controlled situations, is ensuring appropriate supervision and accountability. Only the very best supervisors, with no history of impropriety and clear directions, are needed for these units. Officers assigned to these units must be carefully selected to ensure that they have no previous history of exceeding their authority.

Decisions for staffing these positions within an agency must be made locally, depending on the need and resources available. In many cases, there may be a clear and convincing need but no available resources. The only guidance given here for these positions is to ensure that decisions are based on sound data and not anecdotes. It is also important to ensure that all positions are reviewed periodically, confirming they are still needed and performing in the manner originally intended.

As a side note here, it is interesting, although not surprising, that police and citizens have different views of police use of force. We often see situations where citizens believe that a particular use of force is excessive, but the department and even the courts find that it was reasonable. Police have been trained in the use of force and departments evaluate whether it was appropriate or not by the legal definition provided by the Supreme court in Graham v. Connor (1989). That decision said that an officer's use of force must be judged by determining whether the use of force was objectively reasonable from the perspective of a reasonable officer on the scene, considering the totality of the circumstances, and avoiding the use of hindsight in judgment. Additionally, the evaluation should take into account the fact that officers must make split-second decisions in tense and uncertain situations.

Recent research has shown that citizens frequently take hindsight into consideration when evaluating a use of force. An example might be where an officer used force against an individual with a mental handicap but that person's history was unknown to officer at the time. Citizens also take into consideration the suspects race and the seriousness of the original crime. They believe that a minor crime such as a traffic offense does not warrant an officer using deadly force. Citizens fail to realize the things can escalate quickly.

If a citizen calls the police and wants a stranger removed from their property, or wants to report a minor crime, police are dispatched. The police arrive and ask the person to leave or stop what they are doing. It may be a very minor crime. But they say "No, I don't want to leave, or No, I can do this if I want… it is a free country!" Are the police to simply abandon the encounter and leave? At this point the officers may try any number of persuasion techniques which may also fail. If an actual law has been broken, then an arrest is the last option, and the citizen resists and fights the police. This has now escalated to a serious felony and if the citizen is getting the better of the officer, the officer may resort to deadly force to protect him or herself. Officers did not use force based on the trespass or the minor law violation, it was because they presumably needed to protect themselves during an arrest.

Certainly, this is a simplification., but is intended to illustrate the differences in citizen and police understanding of the use of force by officers. No use of force is pretty. They are typically not like Chuck Norris easily and effectively handcuffing a suspect. Clearly, there have been some horrendous breaches in police use of force in the past few years, and some officers have been held accountable. Officers and police departments, as well city leadership should be aware of these differences when discussing use of force events.

Possible Questions for the Police Department

1. Has the department recently conducted a workload analysis to determine current staffing requirements?

2. What is the current response time to priority one calls?

3. Are officer shift assignments designed to have the most officers working during high-call load times?

4. Does the police department use any non-sworn members to respond to less dangerous calls for service?

5. What is the current clearance rate for index crimes?

6. What ancillary positions exist within the department and are they staffed with sworn or civilian staff?

Chapter 7
Control and Supervision

In recent years many of us have witnessed clear evidence of police agencies and police officers out of control. In most cases, the ultimate cause of failure can be traced back to the lack of leadership, lack of proper control processes, and poor supervision. We can also point to poor hiring choices, poor training, and repeated failure to hold officers accountable for their actions. New police chiefs coming into an agency, even if they are the best and brightest, are saddled with an agency that was built over many years. Bringing in a young very progressive chief into a tradition bound organization can create significant conflict.

Reforming or developing a new department culture with middle managers and supervisors who may fail to share the new vision is extremely difficult. If a city finds itself with a police department in trouble, selecting a chief from outside the department is usually the best option. Finding a candidate with a clear understanding of the police department you want, and with experience in successful organizational change is extremely difficult. It is often made more difficult when a new chief is hired with a mandate for change, yet he or she does not have the ability to hire or appoint their direct reports and staff needed to support it. Nevertheless, it is the chief's job to build and manage the department and be accountable for doing so.

How does a police chief exercise control over a department? They do it by developing a future vision of the department, developing a mission statement that embodies that vision with core values that clarify the department's beliefs. They create control processes with clear and complete policies and procedures. They do it by hiring the best they can find, providing the best training they can afford, the best supervision and disciplinary systems, and by paying attention to everything that's going on in the department. They do it through strategic planning and goal setting that focuses the department's efforts on what is most important. They do it by building audit systems that can identify problem officers and activities before they escalate. And they must continue to do that day in and day out. This is not a once and done process.

Vision

A new chief must first set a vision for the department, with input and assistance from the city manager and council, and members of the department. That vision must be well communicated to every member of the department, along with the rationale of why it was developed. What is a vision? A vision should clearly describe the kind of department and culture the chief wants the department to become. It is typically expressed in the department's vision, mission statement, and core values. In written form, such as in a Vision Statement, a longer and more detailed explanation of the mission and values will help to clarify the meaning. Once in place, the chief can begin making necessary changes to align operations and personnel to meet this vision. Vision and mission statements provide officers with direction when they encounter situations not specifically covered in policy or training.

Policy and Procedure

Police chiefs rarely directly supervise officers in the field, except in very small departments. Therefore, written policy and procedure manuals are needed to ensure all officers are aware of the appropriate methods and procedures to be used in carrying out their duties. State laws often allow officers great latitude in law enforcement, but department policies can further restrict actions when those actions are detrimental to a community. Department policy is essential to ensure all members of the department clearly understand approved and unapproved actions. For example, some police agencies allow officers to pursue a vehicle under any circumstance. In other departments, where population density and the risk of injury or death to uninvolved motorists or pedestrians are high, officers may be limited to pursuing only those where there is clear evidence that the driver is involved or wanted for a violent felony offense.

Policies are only as good as their enforcement. Officers who see supervisors not enforcing certain policies will be reluctant to follow any policy themselves. Chiefs must clearly communicate policy and ensure that supervisors understand the rationale for the policy and enforce even the most disliked policy. This is one of the chief's most difficult tasks. Supervisors are usually selected from the lower ranks of a department and are then put in the position of supervising their former work group. It is very difficult to properly discipline your best friend and colleague that you have worked with for years. Middle managers can also derail attempts at holding officers accountable. Supervisors and managers want to be liked by their work groups and this sometimes allows violations of the policy to go uncorrected.

Most police chiefs build new policies off the back of previous policies and policies from other departments. This is easier and more efficient than building from scratch. But simply taking a policy from another city and changing the name of the department doesn't work. There is no guarantee that the imported policy will fit the department vision, the ideas of city leaders, or even the community. Most police policies are benign and impact only internal activities, but some impact the community at large such as the use of force (including deadly force), stop and frisk, arrest, search and seizure, consent searches, and pursuits.

Police chiefs often do have the greatest technical knowledge regarding policing, and many believe review of these policies by city leadership is neither warranted nor needed. While most city leaders are not experts in either policing or the legal issues surrounding law enforcement, they are usually significantly aware of community preferences. Ensuring your police department policies are consistent with community expectations is critical to building community trust and legitimacy. Department policies that impact the community should be reviewed by city leadership. If objections are raised or questions asked, the chief should be able to provide the reasoning for the policy and the impact of any suggested changes.

Even though most city attorneys are not criminal attorneys, they should be allowed to do a legal review of the policy. Many state accreditation programs and the International Association of Chiefs of Police have model policies that already have had a legal review and can be modified for most departments' use.

Strategic Planning

Police chiefs also direct police operations and focus department activities using strategic plans and objectives. Using strategic plans is an effective manner to focus operations on what is most important to the citizens. It is also a method of controlling the department to restrict activities that are not part of the plans.

Hiring

Hiring the right people is critical. Smaller departments with limited training budgets often try to hire individuals from other jurisdictions because they are already trained. These are called lateral hires. While this may seem like an easy solution, departments need to conduct very thorough background investigations to ensure they are not hiring someone else's problem officer. Background investigations plus both medical and psychological screenings done by professionals who are familiar with policing requirements are an absolute necessity for all applicants. How do you determine if this is being done correctly? The only method is to review a sample of background investigations conducted by the department. This is usually done by either the police chief or the city manager. Reading the state requirements for police background investigations first is advised to determine any weaknesses.

In recent years, a few larger agencies have had to lower their standards in order to fill their ranks. There are multiple cases where this process has created major problems in later years. There is no doubt that some standards can be modified without severe problems. However, department standards should not be lowered when it comes to doing a complete and thorough background investigation, to ensure that the candidate has no previous serious criminal activity, has a good work history, no prior rejection of supervisory authority, and has credible and consistent positive recommendations from personal references and prior employers. The final hiring decision must rest with both the department and the chief. But this process also should be approved by the city manager and council with some form of periodic checking or auditing for compliance.

Training

Appropriate training is also a component of control. Unfortunately, police academies are long, usually at least six months. This training is also intensive with some items being taught and tested in just one week's time, leading to some items being forgotten or dimmed over the course of the entire academy. Most departments require another few months of field training where the recruit rides with a senior officer. Over the course of this training, the recruit is given more and more responsibility for answering calls and conducting enforcement, being evaluated along the way.

At the end of this training there is usually a formal evaluation process where the recruit is either retained or released from employment. Unfortunately, because of the difficulty in hiring and training officers, less desirable officers may be retained just because they need to fill a position. Great care needs to be taken when selecting field training officers because they can completely erase the community-centric training a recruit may have received in the academy. A recruit's greatest desire when graduating the academy is to be accepted by his or her peers as one of the competent "real" police officers. Everyone involved with the hiring process needs to understand that candidates at this point in their career are very malleable.

Another current concern is that police training is too short. Many European countries have law enforcement education programs lasting up to four years. Their curriculums include significantly more instruction in communication skills, de-escalation, and handling mental health crises. While this extensive training is highly desirable by the policing community in the United States, the reality of who will have to pay for this training becomes a stumbling block, coupled with the immediate need for officers, makes this a difficult goal to accomplish.

Unfortunately, some police academies are still teaching older, more traditional models of policing that some senior officers attended some 10 or 20 years ago. But over the years policing has changed significantly. Hopefully, the academies and officers have changed with it. That's why in-service or continuing training is so important to keep senior ranking officers apprised of new processes, procedures and requirements.

Most state governments have some form of governmental unit that dictates the basic requirements for police officers, regulates police academies, establishes basic training requirements, and publishes requirements for continuing training. These basic and continuing training requirements are often developed based on legislative mandates from legislators that believe they have the answer to a particular policing issue. Most of these are well-intentioned and most are beneficial, but they often lack the benefit of recent scientific police research. In other words, current and past academy curriculums and in-service training may not require specific classes even though recent scientific research shows they are needed. Most progressive policing today ensures that officers have relevant training in policing topics that have been born from recent and relevant scientific research.

The Supreme Court, in Monell v. Department of Social Services of New York, allows claims against cities for failure to properly train or supervise officers or employees. The public now expects officers to be highly trained to swiftly solve varied and intricate problems. Detailed training for all these issues is both time-consuming and expensive. In addition to the outright cost of the training, chiefs must also consider who is going to answer the citizen's calls when the officers are attending training.

Providing effective and efficient in-service training is difficult for a number of other reasons. It is not feasible nor effective to hold in-person classes for just one or two officers. The end result is that officers receive much less training than desired or needed. Because of limited experienced instructors, training required by the state or needed by the department may only be offered in that region once or twice a year, with only a few officers from each agency able to attend. Recent studies by the Department of Education determined that online training is just as effective as traditional classroom training and much easier to administer. They even concluded that students did marginally better with online classes. Therefore, cities should consider moving much of their needed instruction to online classes.

Although these items will change and new research will support new and additional training in the future, agencies should ensure their officers have recent and updated training in the following:

Use of force and deadly force. This training needs to be ongoing, It should include both the state's current law and the department's policy regarding the use of force, as well as the use of deadly force. Training should include department instruction on how to use other less lethal weapons such as batons, pepper spray, and electronic control devices (Tasers).

Hands-on defensive tactics. This training ensures that officers learn physical self-protection skills, with guidance on how to reduce reliance on higher levels of force.

Implicit bias. Without labeling officers as being biased, this training explains how individuals' attitudes and beliefs are influenced by their environment and how slowing down incidents, whenever possible, can lead to better decisions.

Data-driven and hot-spot policing. Many officers still operate on the assumption that they should be driving around the community waiting for the next call. Supplying officers with the best research available on crime prevention and interception provides them with the tools they need to impact crime in the community.

Problem-oriented policing (POP). Patrol officers are reluctant to use POP because it is different from their routine. POP offers one of the best methods for impacting future crime and making cities safer.

Procedural justice. The 21st Century Policing report identifies procedural justice as one of the best tools for increasing trust in a community, yet few police departments have adopted the model for field use. Setting this model as a standard for community interactions can increase trust and legitimacy, as well as increase public cooperation in policing incidents.

De-escalation and critical incident training. This training provides officers with valuable communications skills to de-escalate and better handle critical incidents and responses to mental health crises.

Search Warrant Training. This training addresses the requirements for search warrant affidavits, and department policy when executing search warrants. Some departments require higher level supervisory approval for search warrants. Due to some recent events some cities have eliminated no-knock warrants and prohibited executing warrants when it is dark outside.

Constitutional and ethics training. This training ensures that all officers are up to date with current policies regarding constitutional guarantees and professional ethics.

Active Shooter training. This training prepares officers to quickly and effectively respond to active shooter events.

Trauma-informed investigations. New brain research recognizes that trauma changes the way the brain records data and the way individuals can recall data from memory. This training has a significant impact on how and when police officers should question victims of trauma. This training also helps the officer to better understand how trauma can impact victims' memory recall. This approach can have a tremendous effect on citizen perception of the police as they investigate violent offenses.

City leaders and police chiefs need to ensure that their departments maintain a high level of training and cover new areas of police research as it becomes available. Chiefs should also be aware of the specific content of any third-party training providers. Over the years, some third-party provider's training curriculums have tended to make officers more paranoid about self-protection, which could lead to increased use of force. In some cases, these schools may be working against the specific needs of building trust in a community.

Supervision

Selecting the right supervisors and managers is another way for police chiefs to manage and control police agencies. If a new police chief does not have the trust and confidence of supervisors and managers, there will be little change in the department's culture. Cultural change takes place slowly over time as supervisors, managers, and police officers adopt new beliefs provided by a police chief that communicates and empowers the department. Police officers work for their Sergeant. They do not work for the police chief; they work for their sergeant. Most officers seldom see the chief. Their sergeant makes assignments, backs them up in dangerous field situations, teaches and encourages them, disciplines them when necessary, approves their arrests and reports, and completes their performance evaluation.

A sergeant can destroy an officer's reputation on the shift with a single unkind word. It is the sergeant's opinion that is most valued, and if he disagrees with a police chief's direction or vision, there is likely to be very little change. Police chiefs need to actively engage with their line supervisors regularly to ensure they understand and communicate the department's vision and operational strategies to their staff. Many police agencies have collective bargaining agreements. Some even have contracts that limit management's ability to discipline or even move personnel within a department. Police chiefs must have the ability to influence supervisors and, in one way or another, make supervisory changes if needed. Those who consistently thwart the chief's direction must be effectively managed to make meaningful changes or alter organizational culture.

While an internal complaint investigation process (usually called internal affairs) can be used to investigate citizen complaints is both necessary and important, it does not take the place of good supervision. These internal affairs units or staff members seldom do any proactive investigations that might identify problem officers before they damage the department or citizens. Some of today's most egregious failures with policing in our country resulting in the death of citizens at the hands of the police can be traced back to supervisors, managers and chiefs not properly monitoring and holding their officers accountable.

When body cameras were first introduced into law enforcement, departments required supervisors to randomly review a few videos for each of their officers each month, believing this would encourage officers to be more conservative in their approaches to citizens. This review process is actually a very time-intensive and boring job. Unless someone is actively checking to make sure that this is being done, supervisors will likely put this at the bottom of their to-do list and it often fails to get done. When supervisors fail to say to an officer, "That traffic stop you made on Boyton Avenue last week was really well done." Or "Mike, during your interaction with the lady at Walmart last week, you got a little heated. I need you to remember to not get upset with our citizens." When officers realize that their videos are not being reviewed, they will act accordingly. Supervisors not taking action to identify and correct officer behavior is the leading cause of many of our critical incidents today.

Even in small cities reviewing officer's body camera videos can be extremely boring and randomly selecting the videos to review makes the chances of happening to select a video where the officer did something well or in need of correction is minuscule. With the new artificial intelligence revolution, private companies and body camera manufacturers are building systems that automatically scan officer's videos, listening to the audio, and identifying videos in which certain words or phrases are used. Departments can identify the words that often escalate situations and thereby identify videos which may need further review by supervisors and managers.

This lack of supervision is especially true with special crime impact units. These units, even if created to impact crime in city hot spots, have a long history of mismanagement and lack of supervision and accountability. The clear intention of the unit's mission is to impact crime and, therefore, officers assigned begin to believe that the end is worth the means. This noble cause corruption can lead to officers and supervisors bending the rules, cutting corners, and pushing the limits of their authority to show results. Unfortunately, on some occasions, this leads to officers violating the law, abusing citizens, and in some cases, taking their lives. Creating specialized crime impact units should be viewed with caution. If created, they should be staffed with the most reliable supervisors available. Even with the best supervisors possible, closely monitoring their activities should be carried out regularly by upper-level administrators to ensure proper operations.

Staying on Track

Kudos to everyone for hiring what appears to be a competent police chief. The chief has developed a vision and mission statement, issued a new policy manual and strategic plan, as well as revised the hiring and training program. He has studied the staffing issue and requested and received the staffing that is needed, or at least made plans to address it. The new chief has implemented the recommended training and everything is right with the world. Congratulations!

Now all that everyone has to do is sit back and watch the crime rate fall. This situation is like driving a car at 80 miles an hour on the interstate while closing your eyes for a quick nap. Eventually the road will curve, or someone will pull out in front of you. Of course, things will not end well. To avoid a crash, the chief needs to keep his eyes open and constantly make small adjustments as needed. Pay attention and watch the road!

Monitoring Operations

Most police chiefs have some kind of reporting system to tell city hall how the police department is doing. Unfortunately, many city managers and councils have no idea what they should be monitoring or when it is good or bad. Some likely items to report monthly to city hall could include the number of citizen calls, index crimes committed, arrests, citations, complaints against officers, and any unusual incidents.

When a member of council or city manager receives a monthly department report listing 28 index crimes, how do they know if this is good or bad? How does it compare to the local region or state average? Unless someone pulls and examines reports from previous months to show comparisons, those receiving these reports have no idea if the crime is up, down or the same when compared to last month or last year.

Periodic Reporting

One of the biggest problems with monitoring police operations is not receiving the right data, nor understanding what it means. City managers and councils may simply accept the monthly reports from the police department without understanding what they really need or want to know. The lack of knowledge about policing strategies and operations often prevents them from asking detailed questions. There is no requirement that all city managers and council members be experts in policing. Nonetheless, if or when a department goes off the rails, fails to properly respond to citizens, fails to earn their trust, or fails to perform even the most common crime prevention activities, who is to blame? Is it the responsibility of the police chief alone? Or should the manager and council, who never asked any questions, never personally rode with an officer, never requested information nor understood staffing issues, bear some responsibilities, too? Managers and councils should never become involved or even require briefings on details of specific ongoing calls or investigations, but they should be asking for information they need to evaluate the department's performance.

Periodic reporting is one of the primary methods of controlling and monitoring a police agency. However, it only works when receiving the right information. To be sure, measurements and activity reports are important to keep the agency on track. Details regarding the number of citizen calls, arrests, citations issued, training hours, and other things accomplished show that the department is working and performing their basic operations. Analyzing these activities over time can show city leaders that certain activities are being done and whether they are going up or down. Unfortunately, some of these activities may not always produce results.

Why does the police department exist? Is the city willing to fund a police department just to answer calls and arrest violators or should the department try to actually reduce preventable crime? Performance measurements differ from activity reports in that they measure results. If the council and city administration have developed goals for a department's strategic plan, the reported data should include information relating to how these goals are being accomplished. Ideally, police department reporting should include both activities and performance measures to deliver an accurate picture of their ongoing operations.

So, what is the best police reporting system? Unfortunately, it doesn't exist. There are some basic concepts, but each city is very different. Most city managers and city council have slightly different ideas about what needs to be done in their city. Smaller departments have less administrative time available to prepare reports and collect data. While some basic tasks should be reported regularly, the frequency may vary depending on the difficulty of data collection. Designing the best reporting system for a city should start by developing goals for the police department. As goals change over time, whether due to managers or councils who come and go, so should the reporting system change to stay current with these changing circumstances. While every city presumably wants its police department to respond to citizens' calls for service, not all cities have a significant homeless problem or have a goal regarding managing and protecting the homeless. Thus, reporting on the homeless situation may not be relevant to one city as much as it is to another. Of course, the more detail needed in a report, the more difficult and time-consuming it is to collect and report this data.

This can become a real balancing act.

Performance Measures

A good starting place for goal development may be using Goldstein's list of policing goals. While school district and university police departments may have slightly different needs and goals, there are five main outcomes or performance measurements that can apply to all police agencies. Of course, additional performance measurements can be added to meet locally specific goals. The five most common measurements for all police agencies are crime rate, citizen calls response times, accident reduction, department clearance rate for serious crimes, and citizen satisfaction. Some activity measurements can show what is being done in each area, but these performance measurements still must be computed. Since computing some output or performance measurements can be difficult and even complex, cities should consider receiving these reports annually in smaller agencies, or quarterly in larger agencies.

Crime Rate

Historically crime rates have been based on the FBI's definition of index crimes. These crimes include murder, rape, robbery, aggravated assault, burglary, theft, and auto theft. It is not an ideal measurement because it counts many smaller crimes, like shoplifting a five-dollar item from Walmart the same as murder. However, it is nearly ubiquitous among police agencies. It remains to be seen how the new NIBRS system will impact crime rate calculations. The advantage of using a common counting system is being able to compare crime rates to other cities and the larger region or state. Computing a city's crime rate allows one to compare it to previous years, to similar size cities, and state averages. It will be a good monitor for evaluating crime reduction programs being conducted by the police department.

If a police department is using a hot-spot crime reduction model, it may be a good idea to measure preventable offenses or crimes just within the hot-spot boundaries from one period to the next. (Preventable crimes being those that would not likely have occurred if police were seen nearby.) If using Problem Oriented Policing, reporting project results may be beneficial. If the department is using a focused deterrence project, reporting the total number of focused deterrence targets and results during the past year can be very helpful.

Response Time

Response time is commonly measured in the average number of minutes required to respond to emergency and non-emergency calls. Emergency calls are usually defined as calls where a citizen has been injured or is in immediate danger. Officers generally respond to these calls with vehicle lights and sirens on. Most agencies try to respond to emergency calls in under five to six minutes. Generally, the response times can be easily computed using the department's CAD system. These response times are highly influenced by the number of officers available on the street. Increased response times may indicate a staffing shortage, or in some cases, poor supervision or lack of management attention.

Accident Reduction

The main goal for issuing traffic citations is to reduce the number of traffic accidents, injuries and deaths. A monthly report citing the number of minor, injury and fatal accidents, along with year-to-date versus last year-to-date can indicate whether or not this goal is being met. Using appropriate data from accident reports makes it possible to identify high accident locations and times. Targeted enforcement for violations causing these types of accidents and where they occurred can reduce the number of accidents.

Clearance Rate

The total department clearance rate for serious crimes is a measure of how well the department is investigating and solving the crimes that are reported. These numbers can be easily manipulated by individuals within the department and occasionally can be suspect, but they also can show problems within the investigation unit. The unit may not be properly staffed or properly applying case management techniques. Using the FBI's index crimes, smaller departments usually clear more crimes than larger departments. On average, clearance rates can be found in a state's online crime publications. Average clearance rates for most small-to-medium-sized cities can run between 22-26 percent for the total of index crimes. Major cities are much lower, usually 12-15 percent, with some of our largest cities in single digits. Commonly, this is a result of extremely low staffing in the investigative units and, in some cases, very poor management practices.

Citizen Satisfaction

One of the most difficult measurements to determine is citizen satisfaction because it can be influenced by many outside factors, but it is still very important. Most of the time citizen satisfaction is determined through an annual citizen survey of city departments where citizens rank the confidence they have in a department by percentages from excellent to poor. Some cities implement a quarterly survey or insert questionnaires with their water bills. Typically, the response rate is very low, but it may be the only way to evaluate citizen satis-faction. Another possible method is to send direct questionnaires to citizens asking them to evaluate police service for their area. Several cities put a link to an online survey at the bottom of every email issued to citizens by city staff. Whichever method is chosen, the responses must be measurable.

These five performance measurements are about tracking accomplish-ment of strategic plan goals should be computed and reported perhaps quarterly or annually. More detailed monthly reports that include the previous periods' comparative data are reported monthly and are essential for keeping a depart-ment on track. **Appendix C** identifies several types of data that can be included in these monthly reports. Not every agency requires all data suggested, and other data may be specifically needed in your city. Some cities with a competent Information Technology (IT) group have built an online dashboard using many if not all of the data displayed visually and updated daily. Whether a monthly report or an active dashboard, city leaders need to pay close attention to these reports, ask questions, and yes, periodically ride with an officer to see what goes on for themselves!

Possible Questions for the Police Department

1. What are the department's vision, mission and core values?

2. Does the department *use-of-force* policy require de-escalation when time permits?

3. When was the department policy manual last updated and reviewed by the council?

4. What are the current department hiring processes, requirements and disqualification factors?

5. When was the last time officers were trained in x, y and z?

6. Do all supervisors receive supervisory training?

7. Has the department done a training assessment to determine what additional training is needed?

8. Does the department have staff trained in critical incident (handling mental health crises) available on each shift?

9. Does the department have alternatives to sending officers on mental health calls?

10. Does the department have the necessary training resources they need?

11. Does the department utilize body cameras? If so, when is their use required, how long are videos kept, are supervisors required to review videos and when, and how does the department ensure that this is being done?

12. Does the department have any specialized *crime impact units?* If so, how are they supervised?

Chapter 8
Accountability and Reform

Paying attention in a police department means continuously checking to see if things are still working the way they were intended. A chief can't do that adequately by sitting in an office reviewing reports or waiting to answer the next question. They need to see for themselves, ask questions, and analyze the data. Sound like work? It is! But there is no substitute for personal inspections and audits. Regularly compiled data is great for tracking both activities and identifying trends, but ensuring things are being done in the manner desired requires regular inspections and audits. *Don't expect what you don't inspect.*

For instance, your department's monthly activity statistics look fine and are in line with last year's statistics, your performance measures are looking good, and everyone at city hall is happy. In order to get those arrest statistics, one of the detectives has been using an unauthorized and unapproved confidential informant to make cases. He has not independently corroborated the informant's information and has signed arrest warrant affidavits using only the informant's information. Then your department raids an alleged drug house that turns out to be the home of the pastor of the local church and arrests his daughter for selling drugs. Afterwards we find out that the unapproved informant was the daughter's scorned boyfriend.

The detective began using this unapproved confidential informant because it was easier than doing the work required and no one ever checked to make sure the policy on use of confidential informants was being followed. He never saw anyone looking at warrant affidavits or asking questions. The supervisor never reviewed the confidential informant files or payments. How could things go wrong? Many new supervisors will not even know they need to check these things periodically, unless someone from above them checks and asks questions first. Why should they check if no one else is going to check their work?

Crime is down, everyone is working hard, and everyone at city hall is happy. Then, a shooting happens in a nearby town and the gun is recovered. Turns out that it belongs to your police department because it was turned in when a former officer resigned. It was supposed to be in the safe in the department's armory, but something happened. Embarrassing to say the least.

How did it happen? It happened because no one was watching, and no one was checking the department's weapons inventory. Since no one was monitoring the equipment, someone found a way to take advantage. Now the department's reputation is sullied and community trust in the department is damaged.

Monitoring monthly activity reports and performance measurements is necessary, but that is not all. Councils and city managers need to be asking questions about audits and inspections. Police chiefs need to ensure audits and inspections are done to ensure things are continuing to work the way they are intended. Which audits and inspections are needed? That depends on the greatest risks a department faces if something fails.

Departments should conduct their own risk analysis to identify critical issues they may need to audit. However, **Appendix D** provides a list of potential issues that have gotten departments in serious trouble over time, along with their relative importance. The more critical the issue, the more often an audit of that function should be performed. City managers should be asking for copies of police department audits when they are performed. After all, if the city manager is not watching, why should the chief go to that length? Sure, some will because of their personal initiative, but others may let them slide until they have the time to do them.

Police Reform

We have all seen many horrific examples of police officers out of control. Because of this there is a significant movement in our country to reform the police everywhere. In reality, we have been reforming the police for decades. While some improvements have been made, many issues still exist that are more difficult to reform. This is because making positive reform, changing the culture of a department, requires a lot of work, and there are internal pressures within some police agencies that often resist that reform. Most police officers believe they do not need to be reformed. They are competent and dedicated individuals doing a very difficult job. They treat all people with dignity and respect and conduct themselves in an unbiased manner. Daily, we see instances of officers placing themselves in danger to protect the public. No doubt, they all could use and would welcome more training because they want to be good at their job. No one comes to this job to intentionally abuse or kill people. But changes happen. Not to all, but to a few.

Police officers resist this reform movement internally because they do not want to be labeled as a racist. They do not believe that the department needs to be reformed because the great majority of officers they know and see are doing the right things. They do not want to see their department labeled as needing reform. Neither do they want policy changes or training implemented for the whole department when the problem was truly just a few officers. Most likely they do know some officers that need reform, or in some cases even terminated.

No one dislikes a bad police officer more than a good police officer. Getting to that point is more difficult.

Everyone has heard of the code of silence where officers will not rat on fellow officers. This is not just a police problem. People learn about tattling on others in kindergarten. Doctors, lawyers, politicians, and other professions often fail to report their peers for violations of ethics or performance. To some extent, this code of silence still exists in some agencies, but it has decreased significantly in recent years. The reason officers are reluctant to rat on their fellow officers is because their job is inherently dangerous. They do that job with the understanding that if they need help, they can call for assistance and other officers will quickly respond and assist. They fear that if they report another officer, they will be ostracized. Then, if they get into a situation where they need help, no one will come. While this is understood, it cannot be allowed to occur, and many agencies have successfully pushed past this belief. Nevertheless, it remains the job of management to identify and deal with those who fail to live up to their oath.

Previously we have discussed ways to hold a police department accountable for performance – getting the best bang for the citizen's buck, so to speak. Doing the things necessary to control crime and respond to citizen calls for assistance. This requires knowing what you want to see occur, constant monitoring, and ensuring the department knows you are monitoring. It includes receiving periodic reports and making periodic visits to the department to ask questions and think about the responses you receive. It also means holding a chief or manager accountable for not meeting the expectations of the community. This may sometimes mean a change in leadership.

Constitutional Policing

There is another level of accountability that is even more important. This accountability ensures that all members of your department operate in a legal, just, and unbiased manner. We continue to see these failures across our country in recent years. Agencies that embrace and require members to practice procedural justice, agencies that have good supervisiors (that is, supervisors who consistently encourage and ensure their officers are performing legally, and managers who regularly verify proper actions) seldom have problems. Then again supervisors, managers and chiefs cannot simply wait for a citizen to be harmed or complain before identifying problem operations or problem officers.

It is a long and difficult process to be hired as a police officer. In almost every agency, part of that process is some form of an oral board where current members of a department ask an applicant, "Why do you want to be a police officer?" If the candidate answered, "I want to carry a gun and beat up on people," the applicant would be rejected in a heartbeat. But the answer is generally, "I want to help people," or "I want to make a positive difference." This is truly what they want to do.

Once hired and trained, officers in the field are quickly met by situations where someone has been injured and they are unable to develop the legal proof necessary to arrest or prosecute the offender. The officer feels frustrated and angry that they cannot help the victims in these circumstances. They are also influenced by our society's movie heroes who are lauded and admired for bending the rules or doing anything necessary to achieve their understanding of justice. Many officers are able to withstand these pressures and stress, but some will falter unless they are encouraged through effective supervision. Situations in recent years like those in Minneapolis and Memphis do not happen without supervisors and managers and chiefs being either complicit or simply asleep at the switch.

In previous chapters we have discussed what some in this country call "Systemic Racism." In reality, it may more closely be defined as economic discrimination because of the criminal justice system's unequal impact on the poor. Police departments are at the very beginning of the criminal justice system and are basically the "gatekeepers" for entry into the system. There are two different possibilities within a police department that may result in disparate treatment of individuals. One is departmental policies, processes and procedures that encourage or allow the disparate treatment or results to occur. The other is the actions of individual officers, whether intentional or implicit, that may produce disparate results. Departments often fail to take sufficiently detailed looks at their operations to tell if either their policies and operations, or their officers are creating disparate impacts on specific groups in the community.

Departmental Reform

Are there department operations, policies or procedures within your police department that on their face seem perfectly reasonable and effective, but create disparate treatment of some groups in the community? And if there are, do these operations truly make our cities safer? Are there other ways to achieve the same crime control goals? Police departments usually have more operational duties to perform than they can complete, so it is no surprise that detailed investigations into the results of their operations are seldom conducted. But these reviews need to be done to ensure our departments are not inadvertently and unintentionally creating disparate impact. What methods can departments use to identify possible organizational issues contributing to systemic disparate results in enforcement?

Survey Data: Many cities conduct regular surveys of city operations rating major departments like police, fire, parks, and others on a scale. Most police and fire departments usually receive very high ratings for their performance, usually having over 90 percent of respondents rating them good or excellent. If these ratings fall, or if the ratings can be sorted by race or by area of town, and the minority community rates the police significantly lower, then additional investigation may be needed.

Policy Analysis: A periodic review of all department policies should be undertaken to ensure all department policies that impact police/citizen interactions are up to date with best practices. Use of force, choke holds, search warrant execution, duty to intervene, consent searches, the use of pretext stops, and use of intermediate weapons are just a few.

Training analysis: Have all officers received required training in the items identified in Chapter 7, as well as other training required by the state or local department? If officers have not been trained in de-escalation tactics or implicit bias avoidance, their individual performance may result in unintended consequences.

Complaint review: An annual analysis of citizen complaints by type of complaint and by race of the complainant may indicate both individual officer issues, but also department operations or policies that are creating conflict. Does your internal complaint investigation process look beyond the instant complaint? Are these same issues occurring, creating conflict, but not resulting in a citizen taking the time to file a complaint?

Social media comments: If your police department has a website or Facebook page, do you regularly review posted comments? Do the comments indicate problem encounters that were not reported as complaints. Do the comments indicate specific departmental operations that may be problematic?

Arrests and citations by charge and race

By analyzing departmental arrests sorting first by the criminal charge and then sorted by race may indicate areas of disparate impact. There is little that can be done if an arrest results from a victim who was harmed and identifies a particular suspect. But many warrantless arrests are for victimless crimes or crimes against society where officers exercise significant discretion in arrests. Minor drug arrests, disorderly conduct, and some trespass violations, as well as many vehicle equipment violations often show remarkable disparity that cannot be rationally explained. Policy changes on how these offenses are handled can greatly reduce their negative impact on a community. Looking at actual criminal case filings can have the same value reducing disparate impacts. Simply identifying the top ten warrantless arrests in the department may identify potential policy changes.

If you find there are items producing a disparate impact, what are some things you can do? Eliminating disparate impact on minorities or the poor within a police department requires a comprehensive and sustained effort involving changes in policies, practices, training, and organizational culture. Here are some steps police chiefs have used to address these issues:

Acknowledge the Issue: The police chief should publicly acknowledge that some policies and operations within the department are having a disparate impact on minorities and that it is a priority to eliminate this impact. This sends a clear signal that addressing this issue is a top priority.

Community Engagement: Foster open and respectful communication with the community. Establish community advisory boards or partnerships to provide input on policies and practices.

Review and Revise Policies: Conduct a thorough review of existing policies and procedures to identify any that may contribute to any disparities. Implement changes to eliminate these practices and ensure equitable treatment for all individuals.

Training and Education: Provide ongoing training for officers and staff on topics such as implicit bias, de-escalation techniques, and fair policing practices. Training should be mandatory and reinforced regularly.

Data Collection and Analysis: Collect and analyze data on stops, arrests, citations, use of force incidents, and other interactions to identify patterns of racial disparities. Use this data to inform policy changes and hold officers accountable.

Diversify Recruitment: Actively work to increase diversity in the police force through targeted recruitment efforts. A more diverse police force can help build trust and improve interactions with diverse communities.

Implement Body-Worn Cameras: Ensure that all officers are equipped with body-worn cameras to enhance transparency and accountability. Utilize new technology to electronically review and assess officer's body camera video for incidents that need further review based on officer's language used.

Use of Force Policies: Review and revise use of force policies to prioritize de-escalation, proportionality, and alternatives to deadly force. Ensure that officers understand and follow these policies.

EFFECTIVE AND ACCOUNTABLE POLICING

Accountability Measures: Implement clear and transparent mechanisms for reporting and investigating misconduct. Hold officers accountable for violations of policies or civil rights.

Promote Career Advancement: Ensure that opportunities for promotions, leadership positions, and specialized units are available to officers from all backgrounds. This promotes diversity in leadership roles. End use of the number of arrests or citations as part of regular or promotional evaluations.

Collaborate with Experts: Partner with external organizations, academic institutions, and experts in racial equity and policing to develop and implement effective strategies.

Transparency and Communication: Keep the public informed about the steps being taken to address systemic racism. Regularly communicate progress and challenges to build trust.

We talk about operational and policy changes, but what are some examples of changes that can reduce disparate impact? Below are some examples used by some agencies:

- Training officers in the financial impact of arrests on the poor, implicit bias, constitutional and fair policing, and de-escalation.

- Modify policies to require:

    - Arrests as a last resort to solving a problem.

    - No arrest for traffic law offenses except with supervisory approval, DWI, or Warrant.

    - No consent searches without specific supervisory approval. No approval given without driver having prior felony or drug conviction.

    - Eliminate quotas for citations (not traffic stops) and prohibit citations for equipment and regulatory violations unless previously warned at least two weeks prior. No multiple citations on stops. Single hazardous violation citation only.

    - Eliminate the use of the number of citations and arrests for use in personnel evaluations and any promotional considerations.

    - Substitute citation for any misdemeanor non-violent or nonspecific victim offenses.

- Hazardous traffic violations are always grounds for a traffic stop, however prohibit equipment and regulatory traffic stops except in department identified and approved hot spot areas for specific crime control purposes.

- Create policy allowing supervisors and command officers to reverse inappropriate arrests and release individuals without bail or arrest record if arrest was inappropriate (with appropriate controls to prevent corruption.)

- Require supervisory (or centralized unit) review of video of all arrests for on-view misdemeanor offenses, all consent searches, and compare to written reports for consistency.

By taking these or similar steps, a police chief can reduce any disparate impact on marginalized groups and foster a more just and equitable relationship between law enforcement and the communities they serve.

Identifying Problem Officers

Police agencies must pay close attention to these issues on a regular basis to ensure their organizational policies and procedures are not the specific cause of disparate impact on community members. But even when the organization's policies and procedures are neutral and non-discriminatory, the final results of actual operations may still produce higher minority group impacts. In some cases, this is the result of the actions of a few officers, either intentionally or through implicit bias. Identifying these officers and the specific actions that contribute to these problems also requires work that many agencies simply don't do.

Early Intervention Systems

For many years, agencies have been relying on what is known as an early intervention system to identify problem officers. This system is a database of incidents, such as reports of an officer's use of force, sick time, and the number of complaints received from citizens (whether sustained or not). These databases are usually maintained in the department's unit that investigates complaints against officers. When an officer reaches a certain number of these incidents, it triggers an alert. When an alert is triggered, a member of the department, usually the officer's supervisor, needs to investigate the situation to see what may be happening and take whatever actions are needed to set the officer back on track. Unfortunately, these early intervention systems often fail to work as advertised.

In theory, these systems can work, but many times the threshold is set so high that no alerts are ever triggered. In some cases, the incidents tracked are not indicative of potential future problems. In cases where alerts are triggered, supervisors often see their jobs as trying to defend their officers. Additionally, many agencies allow minor complaints, like rudeness or disagreements with an officer's actions, to be handled by the officer's immediate supervisor. While this keeps the supervisor in the loop of controlling officer behavior, if no record of the complaint and its resolution is sent to the Early Intervention System, then valuable data is lost making the system less effective than it could be.

For these systems to work properly the data must be complete and it must be as reliable as possible in identifying officers with the potential for future conflict with citizens. The Chicago Police Department recently implemented a new early intervention system that uses significantly more activity data about the officers including the number of calls answered and warrantless arrests made, and uses a new machine learning algorithm that is more accurate than previous versions. It is important that as much data as possible be entered into the system to improve its ability to predict future potential problems. The National Policing Institute, formerly the Police Foundation, recently published the *Best Practices for Early Intervention Systems* that outlines suggested data to be used in the systems.

The specific data that should be captured can vary based on department policies, legal considerations, and the available resources, but here are some essential data points:

Use of Force Incidents: Record details of any incidents where an officer used force, including the circumstances, level of force, and outcome of the situation.

Complaints and Allegations: Keep track of any citizen complaints or internal allegations made against the officer, along with the nature of the complaint and the investigation outcome.

Misconduct Records: Document any instances of officer misconduct, whether it involves on-duty or off-duty behavior.

Arrests and Citations: Monitor the number and types of arrests made by the officer, as well as any citations issued. Design an alert that compares the individual officer's activity by suspects race compared to the department average for that race.

Body-Worn Camera Footage: Incidents of supervisory review where the officer's actions were corrected by a supervisor.

Training and Performance Evaluations: Track the officer's training history and performance evaluations to assess their proficiency and skill development.

Sick Leave and Absences: Monitor patterns of sick leave and absences, as excessive or irregular time off could indicate underlying issues.

Peer Evaluations: Gather feedback from fellow officers and supervisors to gain insights into the officer's behavior and working relationships.

Community Complaints: Take into account feedback from the community, such as community surveys or outreach programs.

Workload and Shift Schedules: Analyze the officer's workload and shift schedules to determine if stress or fatigue might be contributing factors.

Stress and Mental Health: Consider officer stress levels and mental health indicators as these can influence behavior.

External Factors: Examine external factors that might impact an officer's behavior, such as personal issues or traumatic events.

It's important to implement appropriate data privacy and security measures when collecting and storing this information to ensure the system adheres to legal and ethical standards. Additionally, the data should be used responsibly, and interventions should be focused on support and improvement rather than punitive measures whenever possible. The goal of such a system is to identify officers who may benefit from additional training, support, or counseling to prevent potential issues and promote better policing practices. Early intervention systems improve the ability of supervisors to monitor their officers' performance. Most supervisors in police departments today have more responsibilities and duties than they can usually manage effectively. Constant monitoring and tracking of officer performance is difficult at best, and any system that automatically identifies issues should be welcomed. Early intervention systems are designed to be non-punitive and are intended to assist officers in getting the training or assistance necessary to change their behavior to conform with departmental expectations. Intervention by a supervisor may allow officers to self-correct and address issues before they become larger problems.

Psychologists understand that the best predictor of future behavior is past behavior. Early intervention systems should track all complaints made by citizens, regardless of whether sustained or unfounded, or whether smoothed over by the officer's supervisor. Something happened bad enough to make a citizen call and complain. That needs to be tracked and properly investigated, including watching the video of the incident. When alerts are issued, there needs to be clear procedures on who will address the issues and who will review and approve any actions. As valuable as it is, an early intervention system is not the only step necessary to identify potential problem officers.

There should be no argument that police officers should be treated properly under the law and police policy. The very best police agency in the world is made up of human beings and eventually, someone will make a mistake. When these mistakes happen, ensure the chief and the department have ample opportunity to properly investigate the incident without preconceived ideas or directions.

Communication

Both the police chief and city leadership must constantly remind officers of their commitment to constitutional policing. Most of a police officer's day is not like the action movies you see on television or in the theater. Occasionally, officers must make arrests where individuals do not want to go to jail. When officers are met with this kind of resistance and their authority is not enough to control the situation, using force may become necessary. Like all human beings when involved in a physical struggle, the body dumps adrenalin into the bloodstream. Controlling oneself after such an adrenalin dump now becomes much more difficult – both for the arrestee and the officer.

Some officers take a challenge to their authority personally, and respond inappropriately. Officers are trained not to use excessive force in physical confrontations, and departments have policies forbidding the use of excessive force – yet occasionally it still occurs. When it does, the department must send a clear message with an appropriate response. Police officers know exactly what excessive force is and they know it when they see it. Many departments now have policies similar to the following:

Police officers are prohibited from using excessive or unreasonable force during an arrest or detention of an individual. When resistance ceases, the use of force will cease, and officers will immediately assist the individual with appropriate medical treatment to prevent further injury.

Officers will immediately prevent another officer's inappropriate or excessive use of force against an individual by intervening and stopping the unreasonable use of force and making an immediate report of the incident to a supervisor.

Proof of intentional, knowingly, or negligently violating either of these rules should result in corrective action up to and including termination.

Audits and Analysis

It is easy to identify officers who commit violations of the rules after a citizen comes in to complain or when they show up on the evening news. But how do you find them before they go too far? Besides the early intervention systems, communication and proper supervision being most important, conducting specific audits and inspections can assist.

Every state has some laws that address the resistance to police authority or interfering with police operations. Offenses like aggravated assault on a police officer, resisting arrest, interference with public duties, failure to identify and similar laws. These offenses can become *"contempt of cop"* charges where officers add these charges on an arrest to make it more difficult for an individual to get out of jail or post bond. On occasion, these charges are added to teach the suspect a lesson. Experience shows that officers who are prone to use excessive or unreasonable force may escalate encounters and overuse contempt of cop charges. Most of the arrests on these charges are legitimate. But, without being there at the time or investigating each incident thoroughly, a department may not be able to tell -- so excessive or unnecessary use of force may go unnoticed.

Every field officer usually experiences a few of these very legitimate cases over time. An audit that identifies possible contempt of cop offenses in your state, and counts these arrests sorted by officer over an extended period, can identify officers who produce these arrests at a rate much higher than the average. Arrests made by officers with higher-than-expected numbers could then be reviewed along with body camera data to identify potential issues, which can lead to intervention and additional training, if necessary.

Many agencies have embraced body cameras. While evidence suggests that officers acted properly in most cases, it is hard to believe that some of the horrible incidents we have witnessed in recent years were the first time they have ever happened. Many agencies require supervisors to randomly select and review three incidents for each officer they supervise every month. But how do we know that this is being done? Is that enough? Are there checks to ensure that this is done? If an officer is seen doing something that he or she should not, how is it being addressed? These are questions that should be answered. A few agencies now review video footage of every arrest and the associated paperwork to ensure the video and paperwork match, and that the arrest and transport were proper. Other cities have invested in new technology that reviews all body camera video and identifies those incidents that need further review. Specialized crime-fighting units are especially vulnerable to noble cause corruption and should be monitored closely to ensure proper operation.

Patrol officers will often complain about supervisors micro-managing their activities. Most of the time this is appropriate supervision. Unfortunately, the idea of proper supervision has never been explained to street level officers. Police officers don't get training in supervision until they get promoted to a supervisor's job. In smaller agencies, new supervisors are now required to supervise their friends and prior teammates, making it difficult to hold them accountable. Many supervisors fail to see themselves now as part of management.

Our society has been reforming the police for a long time, but we still see terrible things happen. We get lax in our efforts. Police chiefs, city managers and council members move on. We always seem to be starting over. The lack of consistency and attention allows some officers to believe that they will not be found out and held accountable. Or maybe we did hold them accountable, but the civil service office put them back to work. Sometimes police chiefs quit trying when this happens, and the officer stays on the payroll. People interpret what you care about by seeing what you do. If the supervisor, police chief, city manager, college president, and council members are consistently talking about constitutional policing and taking steps to identify the very few officers who violate their oath, then there will be fewer of these horrific incidents. When this attention stops, whatever gains you have made will disappear. You can't fix this once and be done. It is a continuous process.

Racial Profiling Analysis

Agencies accused of racially profiling individuals typically investigate only the specific instances complained about. Usually, evidence for those arrests or traffic stops had a clear legal justification. Case closed -- no more questions asked. Agencies seldom look for significant patterns of racial profiling. Almost no one looks to see if officers are profiling unless there is a citizen complaint. Many states now require agencies to report data on traffic and pedestrian stops by race, but there is seldom any action taken because there is no universally accepted standard for comparison, and each stop, standing on its own, may be justified by the officer observing a traffic violation. Why then do many percentages of races arrested, stopped, or cited show a significant disparity compared to their presence in the driving population?

There are two possible answers to this question. One is that certain crimes are more easily observed being committed by certain races of people. White-collar and computer crimes do not occur out in the open, so these crimes are not easily observed by police. On the other hand, some street corner drug offenses are observable and are usually committed by members of lower socio-economic groups. Since minorities make up a larger portion of the lower socio-economic groups, minorities tend to make up more of these arrests. Some agencies try to justify their statistics in this way, and some agencies don't even look. There is some evidence in academic studies that support the theory that lower socio-economic groups tend to use violence more to settle arguments, but that discussion needs to be left to the academicians.

The other answer is, using an officer's discretion, the officer made a discretionary decision not to cite or arrest a white violator, but in another instance chose to cite or arrest a minority for the same or similar violation. There is little evidence that this occurs with serious crimes where a victim identifies a suspect, but it can easily occur in minor victimless crimes, such as drug possession or traffic violations. If this second answer is true, the officer's actions may be intentional or a result of some implicit bias. Either way, the result is the same, although it takes a lot more work to discover.

Sample Racial Profiling Analysis								
		White		African American		Hispanic	
	Total	Number	Percent	Number	Percent	Number	Percent
City Driving Population			55.3		28.1		16.5
PD MV Stops	38,453	20,035	52.1	12,458	32.4	5,960	15.5
PD Citations	25765	12,934	50.2	8,889	34.5	3942	15.3
Percent Citations	67	64.6		71.4		66.1	
PD Consent Searches	962	271	28.2	486	50.5	205	21.3
Percent Consent	2.5	1.4		3.9		3.4	

Table 4: This example, similar to that of many agencies, shows data from an annual analysis of agency traffic stops, citations and consent searches used in racial profiling reports. (2023).

Table 4 above provides motor vehicle stop data for a sample department. Many agencies do not provide the percentage data shown here because it makes analysis easier and their numbers don't look good. A city's driving population is whatever comparison standard the department decides to use in order to estimate the driving population. Some cities use population, but many drivers that are at risk of being stopped by the police in a city may not live in the city. There are other standards that cities use including the estimated number of car owners by race or the population of those over age 16. There is no standard method used by all cities. If a city has more than a thousand traffic crashes a year, it might be prudent to consider using the race of the not-at-fault driver in these crashes to create these percentages. Not-at-fault drivers constitute a random sample of individuals quietly driving around the city at all hours who were involved in an accident through no fault of their own.

The total traffic stops, citations, and consent searches are pulled from racial profiling data collection system. In the example above, the percentage of African American traffic stops (32.4%), when compared to the percentage of African American city drivers (28.1%), is not off by much. Many cities might suggest that it is just by chance this year that the minority numbers are slightly higher. However, the 4.3 percent difference of African American stops may be problematic if repeated year after year. This percentage may indicate that some officers, certainly not all, are stopping more African Americans and/or Hispanics than whites.

Looking at the percentage of traffic stops that result in citations certainly gives pause. While 71.4 percent of African American traffic stops result in citations, only 64.6 of white traffic stops result in a citation. It will also be especially difficult to explain or defend when the percentage of African American and Hispanic consent searches (3.9% and 3.4 %) is more than double the rates for whites (1.4%.)

Most racial profiling reports present only the total department data on traffic and pedestrian stops. Some states, in some cases due to the urging of police officer unions and associations, have prohibited departments from releasing individual officer statistics for fear of labeling the officer a racist. Even so, that does not mean that a department cannot look at this data internally. Looking at an individual officer's traffic stops, citations and consent searches when sorted by race, can identify individual officers whose minority traffic activity is significantly higher than the averages for all field officers (see **Figure 5**).

		African American	Asian	Caucasian	Hispanic	Native American	Total
Individual Officer Motor Vehicle Stops by Race							
Department Total MV Stops		18.9%	15.3%	50.0%	15.6%	0.2%	
Officer 1	MV Stops	351	59	227	196	0	833
	Percent	42.1	7.1	27.3	23.5	0.0	100.0
Officer 2	MV Stops	93	17	173	129	0	412
	Percent	22.6	4.1	42.0	31.3	0.0	100.0
Officer 3	MV Stops	239	17	266	151	0	673
	Percent	35.5	2.5	39.5	22.4	0.0	100.0
Officer 4	MV Stops	112	8	118	75	0	313
	Percent	35.8	2.6	37.7	24.0	0.0	100.0

Table 5: *A sample analysis showing some officers are much higher than the department average in stopping minorities.*

When officers are identified in this manner, further investigation is needed because there can be very legitimate reasons for this disparity. The officer may be working in a predominantly minority area, or he may be on a special investigative assignment that may artificially create a higher minority percentage. Still, officers seldom make traffic stops or arrests only on their beat. Recent advances in mapping software readily allow arrest or traffic stop data to be plotted using addresses in the department's CAD or records management systems. The point is, having a higher percentage of minority arrests or traffic stops versus the department average does not automatically indicate a problem officer – but it does need to be examined further.

Consent Searches

Looking at the number of consent searches conducted by each officer by race, and the results of those searches, may also indicate a need for intervention. Officers and chiefs need to understand that when an officer asks for consent to search a vehicle, the officer is basically saying to the driver, "I think you are a crook." No amount of sugar coating is going to change that perception. To a citizen who has already been to prison, this probably is not a big shock. However, to the average citizen who has never had contact with law enforcement, it is a tremendous insult and cause for concern. Soon, all their family and friends will hear about it.

Examining an officer's use of consent searches and their individual hit rate is very instructive. Hit rate is the percentage of consent searches that result in some kind of contraband (guns, drugs, evidence of a crime) that would not have been found except for the search. Some officers with a very low hit rate may be using the consent search as a fishing expedition. Average hit rates are typically between 20-30 percent.

Looking at the actual number of consent searches and the actual contraband or money recovered from these searches may lead some departments to restrict their use. Before allowing an officer to request a consent search, some agencies may want to consider placing extra requirements on the search. This may include whether the person involved in the search has a prior record for drug offenses, or for the officer to secure supervisory approval. Officers with a higher percentage of consent search requests of minority versus white drivers should require further supervisory investigation, increased monitoring, and corrective action, if necessary.

Court Citations

Looking at actual court citations or doing audits can identify other issues. When officers approach a violator, it is usually the officer's discretion whether to cite or release the citizen with a warning. How this is done depends on a myriad of factors, such as how dangerous is the violation to other drivers, the driver's acceptance of guilt and understanding of the potential danger to other drivers and, in some cases, although inappropriate, the violator's reaction to the police authority. Looking at traffic stops and citations together can show the percentage of stops that result in citations by officer, and by violator race, which could identify another problem area.

When making traffic stops, some officers may choose to issue a single citation, even though multiple violations were observed. For instance, the officer sees a vehicle run a red light, so he makes the driver pull over. It turns out that the driver does not have his driver's license with him, his inspection sticker is out of date, and the vehicle license plate is expired by a month. Some officers will give a citation for the red light only because it is the most hazardous offense. The same officer may then issue a verbal or written warning for the other offenses.

Some officers may feel compassionate towards the driver because they have four screaming toddlers in the back seat, thus releasing the driver with only a verbal warning, or cite the least expensive violation. Similar to the contempt of cop arrests discussed earlier, if the driver does not respond to the officer's authority in a manner the officer feels appropriate or for other reasons, the driver may be cited for all four violations. Looking at instances of multiple citations by officer and by race may also identify problems. As discussed earlier, these additional fines can drive some citizens deeper into poverty where they cannot escape.

Analysis of the *type* of citations being issued can also be instructive, both from a department and individual officer basis. Citations for hazardous violations have an impact of reducing deaths and injuries from accidents. Equipment violations, such as no motor vehicle inspection sticker, license plate expired, and a single brake light out, are less so. Because of the racial disparity when issuing citations, a few departments prohibit officers from issuing such citations, preferring instead to issue a warning. A subsequent citation is issued only if the driver was previously warned. Audits of this nature also identify officers that make few traffic stops and issue few citations. This is a separate, but no less important issue for department performance and supervision.

These same issues regarding officer discretion can occur in custodial arrests as well. Analysis of department arrests and each officer's arrests by suspect race and type of crime can find patterns that would recommend additional investigation. Analysis of individual officers' traffic stop, citation, and arrest data can reveal problem areas, if a department takes the initiative to look.

Indications of disparity in traffic stops, citations, searches or arrests do not automatically predict a future use of force, but may predict more future inappropriate stops, which are also of concern. Traffic stops are one of the most frequent police contacts with citizens, and one that occasionally leads to the use of force. These audits with significant findings, combined with an effective early intervention system, can assist agencies and cities in identifying and correcting problem behavior.

Counseling Officers

Discussing the results of an audit of this nature with an officer whose numbers are out of the norm can be quite difficult for supervisors. Officers will always state that they only stop the violators they see. When officers who stop a significantly higher percentage of minorities are identified, supervisors should attempt to determine the reasons why before talking with the officer. Supervisors need to examine the stop locations, violations cited, whether a search was conducted, what percentage of searches were consent searches (by race) as well as the types of cars stopped. If no obvious reason for the disparity is determined, the supervisor might well review videos of the stops to see if they can determine what is happening. If no clear explanation is determined, the officer should be asked for an explanation.

The officer may not know the reason but will claim it is just what he saw. It is possible that his actions are the result of some form of implicit bias. Still the numbers do need an explanation, and the explanation needs to be verified. These numbers along with some of the issues identified earlier in discussions of the early intervention system may point to an officer in trouble. In fact, these types of audit results may need to become part of an early intervention system. How the department handles officers in these situations can range from counseling, to additional training in constitutional policing, implicit bias and department policy, or to transfer to non-enforcement activities.

How chiefs and supervisors handle data that is developed through these types of audits can be critical to officer morale. If statistics show that an officer stops twice the percentage of African Americans than other officers, it should not be automatically assumed that the officer is a racist. All officers, especially those who are aggressive in crime control activities, have a chance of being involved in some critical incident where they may be forced to use their weapons. If in this process a citizen is killed, the department and officer can expect a wrongful death lawsuit. The plaintiff's attorneys in these cases can request this same activity and traffic stop data through discovery and identify the same issues.

Without explanation, these racial inequity issues might indicate to a jury that an officer appears to be a racist. Providing data to the officer, explaining the concern, examining his or her explanations, and attempting to resolve an issue benefits the officer, the department and the citizens. Providing this data to officers who are operating out of the norm, will soon become known to other officers in the department. When this happens, it conveys to those officers that the department takes these issues seriously. Just by the mere fact that officers are being asked questions about these issues can lead officers to self-correct. Continuous out of the norm performance year after year, if not justifiable and after being questioned about the issue, may indicate larger problems for some officers. Usually only a handful of officers are responsible for causing a department's racial profiling report to be significantly out of alignment with its driving population.

If an officer who has been identified as out of the norm has worked day and night shifts during the period under review, it may be possible to further investigate whether race played a part in the traffic stop. Known as the veil of darkness, the department can examine whether the officer's stops were less discriminatory during the hours of darkness because the officer would be less likely to discern the race of a driver at night.

Doing these types of audits, contempt of cop audits, traffic stops by race and by officer, consent search by race and by officer, and citation issuance by race and officer, along with other early intervention system data and activity reporting by can assist department managers in identifying problem officers. Dealing with problem officers individually wins the support of the rank and file because most support correcting or ridding the department of these officers. When problem officers are identified and their behavior cannot be explained, what can be done to intercede and encourage proper behavior? Should the officers identified in these audits and early intervention system alerts be subjected to increased monitoring? Absolutely. It should not be just an option; it should be an obligation. Clearly, additional training can help. Reassignment is always another option. Other ideas include:

- Require notifying a supervisor and the supervisor responding to every use of force by the officer

- Requiring the supervisor to review body cam video on every traffic stop, use of force, and arrest by the particular officer

- Requiring supervisory approval of any consent search request prior to the search

- Requiring supervisory approval of any arrest prior to arrest

Only officers identified as needing this level of supervision should be subjected to these measures. Implementing these measures department-wide can be detrimental to officer morale, reduce their initiative, and be overly burdensome for supervisors. Departments could implement the video review of all arrests and all use of force incidents as a matter of practice to ensure proper operation. Larger departments might consider a separate full-time unit staffed with two or three supervisors. These departments might even require new supervisors to spend time embedded in the unit to learn how to do video reviews of officer activity. Departments can design anonymous reporting systems where officers can report an incident and have department management initiate review of the incident to prevent the reporting officer from being blamed.

If a department is not pursuing these types of audits, how do city management or city councils encourage their use? Usually, elected city council members and school or university boards are only policy-making authorities. They should not have access to an individual employees' personnel or performance records. Normally, only the chief, city manager, or superintendent should have access to an individual's employee data. However, governing bodies can require that this information be reviewed, receive report results (without individual employee names), ask what was done to correct the situation, and require the same audit a year later to see if the corrective action was effective. Reforming and holding police departments accountable by eliminating systemic discrimination requires these types of measures.

By recognizing these issues and providing your police chief with both clear direction and the support and assistance necessary can have a tremendous effect. No one hates a bad cop more than a good cop. Professional police officers who still have the desire to protect and serve will perform in a manner that will make any police agency proud. Just sitting back and expecting the police chief to do this alone can have very disappointing results. To create a police department that your city deserves, you need to be part of the solution.

Accreditation

There are two main sources of Law Enforcement Accreditation, national and state. The Commission on Accreditation for Law Enforcement Agencies (CALEA) is the national accreditation body, and most states have individual state accreditation programs. While CALEA is a non-profit organization, its cost is significantly higher and the internal cost to agencies seeking accreditation is usually much greater. CALEA has over 500 standards, and agencies must provide at least two proofs of compliance a year for each standard. This often requires full-time staff plus significant work within an agency developing and maintaining proofs each year. Still, if you have the financial ability, the national accreditation process has a great reputation.

State accreditation programs are typically run by either the state Police Officer Standards and Training (POST) agency, or the state's Police Chiefs Association. These programs usually have fewer standards, but these standards are what chiefs in that state believe are necessary to have a good police department. They cover critical issues and are specific to that state's criminal laws. Often, they are less expensive and usually do not require a full-time staff to achieve or maintain their programs. Many cities are seeing the benefits of being dually accredited (CALEA plus their state program).

Why should a department become accredited? All accreditation programs require written policies for critical department functions and operations. These policies are then reviewed by outside expert assessors that require changes if the policy does not meet the law or their standards. Before an agency is accredited, it must submit proof that they meet all the standards. This proof is reviewed by police professionals and the departments undergo an on-site inspection of their operations.

Additionally, the agency must submit all policy or operations changes annually for review and undergo another on-site inspection every three or four years. What does that do? It assures city leaders and citizens that the department has the necessary policies and control functions in place. It does not mean that the department will never make a mistake, and it does not mean that it is operating efficiently or effectively. Very few accreditation programs measure outcomes. While some programs require reporting progress on established goals, there is no requirement for any specific crime reduction goals.

Accreditation agencies are one of the best places to find law enforcement best practices. Other organizations that provide policing best practices include the National Institute of Justice (NIJ), The Department of Justice Community Oriented Policing (COPS) Office, The International Association of Chiefs of Police (IACP), the National Sheriffs Association (NSA), The National Organization of Black Law Enforcement Executives (NOBLE), the Police Executive Research Forum (PERF), the National Policing Institute, and the Rand Corporation.

Accreditation does a good job of ensuring that an agency has policies and procedures in place that will reduce its overall risks. In fact, some states' police liability insurance carriers have reduced the rates of accredited agencies. While accreditation is highly recommended and beneficial, it cannot take the place of an active and engaged city management team and governing body.

Possible Questions for the Police Department

1. What audits and inspections do you conduct regularly?

2. Has the department conducted any analysis of departmental operations to determine if any policies or operations create a disparate impact on minority members of the community?

3. Does the department have an early intervention system for identifying potential problems with officers? If so, what are the components? What will be done if the system generates an alert?

4. Does the early intervention system track ALL complaints, even those unfounded or disposed of by a supervisor?

5. Has the department conducted an audit of individual officers' arrests, traffic stops, citations, or consent searches by race to determine if any officers are outside the department norm?

6. How does the department identify officers with potential community interaction problems before an incident or citizen complaint?

7. How many consent searches are conducted by the department and what is the racial makeup of those searched? What is the *hit-rate* for each group? Are officers required to tell citizens they have the right to refuse a consent search?

8. Is the department accredited by both a state and national accreditation body?

Chapter 9
Summary

In those cities that have experienced a police tragedy, we often find the Department of Justice intervening with an investigation. These investigations are quite intense and often include many of the audits described in this book. Reading a multitude of these reports will show that they always find the city has had a lack of resources, deficient training, substandard facilities and equipment, inadequate support and supervision, and supervisory failure to correct misconduct. Who is responsible? Is it the police chief alone?

We discussed what police departments should be doing and what works in policing. We discussed methods for figuring out the number of officers needed to do the things desired by city management and council (or superintendent and school board, and others), and the periodic reporting systems and audits needed. We discussed ways police departments can identify problem officers before the worst happens. If you have not been doing these things, where do you start?

The primary decision that drives all future decisions is what the citizens and their representative council or board want their police department to be doing. When the opportunity presents itself, the top administrator must raise the issue and allow time for discussion, perhaps in a work session. Members of the council or board must first be educated about some of the things discussed here such as staffing and various policing options, and their responses noted. The administrator needs to meet with the current police chief to discuss what the council desires. If a chief's vacancy exists, the administrator needs to ensure that the incoming chief has the experience or willingness to tackle the issues identified.

- Over the coming months or perhaps next year, the administrator and chief should work together to:

- Review or establish a departmental vision, mission, and core values.

- Develop a strategic plan to accomplish the goals set by the council.

- Conduct a staffing study to determine appropriate staffing to accomplish the strategic plan.

- Request the council to review critical operational policies and procedures of the department. The chief of police should be prepared to defend the reasoning behind the policies and willing to make changes requested by the council unless prohibited by law.

- Develop and implement periodic reports designed to allow management and council to see progress toward goals.

- Develop a schedule of audits and inspections that the department can carry out.

- Develop necessary budget requests to fund personnel or items needed to achieve department goals.

The administrator and council should make personal visits to the department, express support for the department and its activities, and become familiar with department operations.

If funding is not available, the administrator and chief should work together to determine the priority of services and activities that are paramount and make the best use of the resources given.

Not all cities are able to afford the police department they want. However, citizens, city councils and city managers need to be assured that their police department is doing the best it can with what it has been given. Developing reasonable periodic reporting and auditing, asking questions, as well as making personal visits can ensure improved and accountable operations.

REFERENCES

Amendola, Karen L. and Davis, Robert C. "Best Practices in Early Intervention System Implementation and Use in Law Enforcement Agencies." National Police Foundation. (November 2018) https://www.policinginstitute. org/wp-content/uploads/2019/03/EarlyInterventionSystem_10.26.pdf

Braga, Anthony A., Brandon C. Welsh, and Cory Schnell, "Can Policing Disorder Reduce Crime? A Systematic Review and Meta-Analysis," *Journal of Research in Crime and Delinquency*, Vol. 5., No. 24, 2015, pp. 567–568.

Bushey, Keith D., 1982. *"Sobering thoughts for Municipal Officials… The Consequences of Hiring a Weak Police Chief".* Public Management (International City Managers Association) March 2002.

Carton, Samuel, Jennifer Helsby, Kenneth Joseph, Ayesha Mahmud, Youngsoo Park, Joe Walsh, Crystal Cody, Estella Patterson, Lauren Haynes, and Rayid Ghani "Identifying Police Officers at Risk of Adverse Events." University of Chicago, 2015.

Connors, Edward, and Barbara Webster. Transforming the Law Enforcement Organization to Community Policing. Washington, DC: National Institute of Justice, 2001.

Center for Evidence-Based Crime Policy, George Mason University. *"What Works in Policing."* https://cebcp.org/evidence-based-policing/what-works-in-policing/research-evidence-review/

Chu, James (2001). Law Enforcement Information Technology: A Managerial, Operational, and Practitioner Guide. CRC Press.

Eck, John E., Chainey, Spencer, Cameron, James G., Leitner Michael, and Wilson, Ronald E. 2005. Mapping Crime: Understanding Hot Spots. Washington, DC: U.S. Department of Justice, National Institute of Justice

EEOC (Equal Employment Opportunity Commission.) "Advancing Diversity in Law Enforcement. Washington, DC: Equal Employment Opportunity Commission, 2016.

Federal Bureau of Investigation, Washington DC, July 2019. *A Guide to Understanding NIBRS.* United States Department of Justice, Federal Bureau of Investigation, 2019.

Federal Reserve, Board of Governors, Washington DC, May 2023, Survey of Household Economics and Decisionmaking in 2022.

Fisher-Steward, Gayle. Community Policing Explained: A Guide for Local Governments. Washington, DC: Office of Community Oriented Policing Services, 2007.

Fridell, Lori Richardon, Dustin Marier, Chris. The Use of Force "Reasonableness Divide" The Police Chief June 2023Goldstein, Herman, 1990. *Problem-Oriented Policing.* New York, NY: McGraw-Hill Publishing.

Kelling, G., Pate, T., Dieckman, D., & Brown, C. E., 1974. *The Kansas City preventive patrol experiment.* Washington, DC: National Policing Institute. https://www.policinginstitute.org/publication/the-kansas-city-preventive-patrol-experiment/

Lentz, Susan A.; Chaires, Robert H., 2007. "The Invention of Peel's Principles: A Study of Policing "Textbook" History." Journal of Criminal Justice. 35 (1): 69–79.

Lum, Cynthia, Koper, Christopher S. and Telep, Cody W. "The Evidence-Based Policing Matrix," *Journal of Experimental Criminology* 7, no. 1, March 2011.

McCabe, James, PhD. *"An analysis of police department staffing: How many officers do you really need?"* Center for Public Safety Management White Paper. International City/County Managers Association.

McCampbell, Michael S. The Collaboration Toolkit for Law Enforcement: Effective Strategies to Partner with Law Enforcement. Washington, DC: Office of Community Oriented Policing Services, 2010.

Morgan, Rachel E., Truman, Jennifer L. 2019. *Criminal Victimization, 2019.* U.S. Department of Justice, Office of Justice Programs.

Natapoff, Alexandra. Punishment without Crime. 2018 New York, NY., Basic Books 2018

Noble, Jeffrey J., and Geoffrey P. Alpert. Managing Accountability Systems for Police Conduct: Internal Affairs and External Oversight. Long Grove, IL: Waveland Press, 2009.

PERF (Police Executive Research Forum). Guiding Principles on Use of Force. Critical Issues in Policing Series. Washington, DC: PERF, 2016.

National Institute of Justice, "Racial Profiling and Traffic Stops," January 9, 2013. nij.ojp.gov:
https://nij.ojp.gov/topics/articles/racial-profiling-and-traffic-stops

President's Commission on Law Enforcement and Administration of Justice, 1967. The Challenge of Crime in a Free Society, Washington, DC: Government Printing Office.

President's Commission on Law Enforcement and Administration of Justice, 1967. *Task Force Report: The Police.* Washington, DC: U.S. Government Printing Office.

President's Task Force on 21st Century Policing, 2015. "Final Report of the President's Task Force on 21st Century Policing". United States Department of Justice. *Office of Community Oriented Policing Services.*

Scott, Michael S., and Stuart Kirby. Implementing POP – Leading, Structuring, and Managing a Problem-Oriented Police Agency. Washington, DC: Office of Community Oriented Policing Services, 2012.

Skogan, Wesley, and Frydl, Kathleen, eds., *Fairness and Effectiveness in Policing: The Evidence*, Washington, D.C.: National Academies Press, 2004.

S. Walker, G. P. Alpert, and D. J. Kenney. Early warning systems: Responding to the problem police officer. US Department of Justice, Office of Justice Programs, National Institute of Justice, 2001.

Taylor, Ralph B., *Breaking Away from Broken Windows*, Boulder, Colo.: Westview Press, 2001.

United States Department of Health & Human Services, Substance Abuse and & Mental Health Servs. Admin., 2021, National Survey on Drug Use & Health (NSDUH), at table 1.27B.

United States Department of Justice, Bureau of Justice Assistance, 2012. *Reducing Crime through Intelligence-Led Policing*. U.S. Department of Justice, Office of Justice Programs.

United States Department of Justice Civil Rights Division, 2023. Investigation of the Louisville Metro Police Department and Louisville Metro Government, Washington, DC.

United States Department of Justice, COPS Office (Office of Community Oriented Policing Services). Law Enforcement Best Practices: Lessons Learned from the field. Washington, DC, 2019. https://cops.usdoj.gov/

United States Department of Justice, COPS Office (Office of Community Oriented Policing Services). Building Trust between the Police and the Citizens They Serve: An Internal Affairs Promising Practices Guide for Local Law Enforcement. Washington, DC: Office of Community Oriented Policing Services, 2009. https://cops.usdoj.gov/

United States Department of Justice, COPS Office (Office of Community Oriented Policing Services). Problem-Solving Tips: A Guide to Reducing Crime and Disorder Through Problem-Solving Partnerships. 2nd edition. Washington, DC: Office of Community Oriented Policing Services, 2011. https://cops.usdoj.gov/

United States Department of Justice, COPS Office (Office of Community Oriented Policing Services). Community Policing Defined. Washington, DC: Office of Community Oriented Policing Services, 2012. https://cops.usdoj.gov/

Van Kirk, Marvin L., Chief of Police,1977. Response Time Analysis. Kansas City Police Department, (46852NCJUS).

Walker, Samuel, Geoffrey P. Alpert, and Dennis J. Kenney. Early Warning Systems: Responding to the Problem Police Officer. Washington, DC: National Institute of Justice, 2001.

Walker, Samuel, Stacy Osnick Milligan, and Anna Berke. Supervision and Intervention within Early Intervention Systems: A Guide for Law Enforcement Executives. Washington, DC: Police Executive Research Forum, 2005.

Wilson, James Q.; Kelling, George L., March 1982. "Broken Windows: The police and neighborhood safety". The Atlantic Monthly.

Wilson, O. W., and Roy McClaren, 1977. *Police Administration*. 4th ed. New York, NY: McGraw-Hill Publishing.

Wilson, R.E. and R.S. Everett. 2004. Targeting Violent Crime in Small Communities: A Spatial Data Analysis. Unpublished research. Washington, DC: U.S. Department of Justice, National Institute of Justice

APPENDIX A: Current Patrol Uncommitted Time

The below computation uses data available from the city payroll system to determine how many hours officers are at work and the actual number of hours they are doing police work. The computation also uses data from the department's CAD system to determine the amount of time officers spend handling citizen-generated calls and related activities. The remaining time not being used for call responses is *uncommitted time*. **Chapter 2** discusses the impact of not having sufficient uncommitted time and includes less proactive police activity, fewer traffic stops, the inability to impact crime, and increased response times. This data is entered into the form at the end of this appendix.

The below processes and formulas can be built into an Excel Spreadsheet if desired and can be used repeatedly when new data is developed. Accuracy can be increased by increasing the detail of the data used.

Data entry items

Line 1: Shift length

Patrol shift length in the number of hours in a shift, usually 8, 10, or 12 hours. This will be used to determine how many days an officer works a patrol shift during the year.

Line 2: Current number of patrol officers

This computes the total number of officers who regularly respond to calls for service.

Line 3: Gross paid hours per year

This is the total number of hours that an officer is designed to work during a year. (For example, 26 two-week pay periods of 80 hours = 2080 hours)

Line 4: Average voluntary hours off per officer

This averages the number of hours from personnel time records. Even if in FMLA status, a 12-month payroll report should be used to determine the total number of vacation hours, holiday and compensatory time taken by officers assigned to call-answering duties. Next divide this total by the number of call-answering officers to obtain the average hours off.

Line 5: Average sick hours used per officer for previous year

The average number of hours from personnel time records, even if in FMLA status.

Line 6: Average administrative hours off

Averages are from personnel time records that include injury, jury duty, military leave, quarantine, death in family leave, and suspension time. Compute total a divide by number of patrol officers to obtain average.

Line 7: Average training hours per officer for the previous year

Average hours of training per year for each officer, including scheduled schools and in-service training.

Line 8: Average patrol officer hours at work per year

This is computed by subtracting lines 4, 5, 6, and 7 from line 3.

Line 9: Average number of shifts each officer is present for work

This is computed by dividing line 8 by line 1. This is the number of shifts a patrol officer is expected to be at work during a year.

Line 10: Estimated administrative time per shift per officer

Even when an officer is at work, his full shift is not spent doing productive police work. This calculation estimates an officer's average amount of unrecoverable time per shift used for briefing, meals, breaks, court, vehicle maintenance, and other individual administrative activities. (This is usually 1.5 for 8-hour shifts, 2 for 10-hour shifts, and 2.5 for 12-hour shifts, but each department should refine these estimates based on the department's operation.)

Line 11: Total administrative time at work per officer per year

This is computed by multiplying line 9 by line 10. It produces the total time an officer spends doing administrative activities (not police work, but still required or allowed) for the entire year.

Line 12: Total hours each officer as available for police work each year

This is computed by subtracting line 11 from line 8. This is the gross paid hours minus the time off from work (vacations, holidays, sick time and training, etc.) and minus the non-police administrative activities (shift briefings, meal breaks, vehicle maintenance, etc.) that are required when at work. This leaves the total amount of time the average officer has each year to conduct police work. The actual police work includes answering citizen calls and proactive officer-initiated actions.

Line 13: Total patrol officer hours available for police work for the year period

This is computed by multiplying the number of officers (line 2) by the average number of officer hours available (line 12). This is the total number of patrol officer hours available for the year.

Next, we need to use CAD data to determine the amount of time required to answer citizen-generated calls for service and related activities.

Line 14: Citizen-generated calls for service dispatched in previous 12 months

Most departments assign incident numbers to every police activity including officer-initiated activities such as traffic stops and jail checks. While this is police activity, it does not accurately indicate citizen call service requirements. This number must be the actual number of citizen-generated calls from citizens who were dispatched to field elements and should not include any officer-generated activity. It should _not_ include traffic stops, jail checks, business checks, or other non-call-related activities. Many CAD systems can produce this data by selecting the call source (such as 911 or administrative line and not officer). If not, produce a list of all incidents in the last 12 months by type of call (accident, assault, burglary, etc.) with the total calls of each type and a total. You can then identify the types of incidents that are officer-generated (such as traffic stops) and remove them from the total.

Line 15: Average time on call for all calls for service

Average time on call is obtained from CAD data for just the citizen-generated calls. Enter as a percentage of one hour. Absent reliable data from the CAD system, use between .66 and .75. On average, most agencies' actual data for officer time on call ranges between 40 and 45 minutes per call.

Greater accuracy: To achieve greater accuracy for your specific agency, some CAD systems can produce the total time spent on call for all units assigned to all calls. (In most cities roughly 40-50 percent of calls require two officers and about 6-8 percent require three or more. Some CAD systems track these times separately and can provide more accurate data for the total hours spent handling citizen calls. Dispatch supervisors and managers can query their systems to produce accurate data for the number of citizen-generated calls and total unit time on these calls. If the city has an IT unit, staff members can be called upon to provide accurate data using CAD systems.

Line 16: Computed total time on call

Total time on call is computed by multiplying line 14 by line 15. It produces the total time officers actually spent during the previous 12 months responding to citizen-generated calls for service. Other duties required when answering citizen-generated calls include writing reports and booking prisoners. That time is captured below.

Note: If the department can track overtime by the cause of the overtime, then the number of hours of late relief overtime due to a citizen's call for service can be added to this total. All overtime should not be added due to it being used for many other reasons.

Line 17: Number of custody arrests made in previous 12 months

This data may be provided by the CAD or records management systems, or even a jail management system. Use the most accurate data possible and, if possible, use only those resulting from citizen-generated incidents for the greatest accuracy.

Line 18: Estimated average transport and booking time per prisoner

This time will vary significantly between departments depending on whether the department has an internal jail, or they must drive a prisoner to the county jail plus the distances involved. Field supervisors and officers should be queried, and sample data collected from the CAD system to estimate the average. Drunk driving arrests often require longer booking processes due to requirements for using an intoxilyzer or blood draws, but an accurate average can be developed from CAD data. Enter as a percent of one hour (45 minutes = .75 or an hour and a half = 1.5).

Line 19: Computed total time on prisoner-related activities

This is computed by multiplying line 17 by line 18 and is the total time spent on booking prisoners from citizen-generated calls.

Line 20: Total reports written in the previous 12 months

This data is obtained from the department's records management system.

Line 21: Estimated average time to complete report

Most departments do not capture report writing time in their CAD system. If not, this must be estimated by field supervisors and officers. It is remarkable that in previous staffing studies involving multiple agencies the report writing time appears to be similar, usually 45 minutes per report or .75 of an hour. If more accurate data is not available from your CAD system, use .75.

Line 22: Computed total time completing written reports

This is computed by multiplying line 20 by line 21.

Line 23: Estimated ancillary non-police duties in the previous year

Some police agencies have their police officers doing other activities not

100

specifically related to police work, such as transporting municipal court revenue to the bank, locking and unlocking city halls and libraries, and performing bailiff duties in the municipal court. These activities take officers away from citizen call-answering duties as well as proactive officer-initiated and crime prevention activities, which some administrators tend to overlook. Department staff can closely estimate the total time needed to perform these activities and enter here the total number of hours spent in a year on these ancillary activities.

Line 24: Total time handling citizen calls and ancillary duties

This is computed by adding lines 16, 19, 22, and 23.

Line 25: Percentage of available officer time handling calls and ancillary duties

This is computed by dividing line 24 by line 13. This will result in a decimal under 1.0 (hopefully) and if multiplied by 100, will be the percentage of available officer time currently being used to handle citizen-generated calls and ancillary duties.

Note: If this number is greater than 1.0, then some entered data is inaccurate. That would mean that some calls are not being answered. As stated, police agencies often self-adjust to handle the workload. If the number is greater than one, and all calls are being answered, it may be that officers are not spending as much time on each call as the data entered indicates, or the time of booking prisoners and writing reports is less.

Line 26: Percentage of available officer time uncommitted

This is computed by subtracting line 25 from 1.0 or (100 if you multiplied by 100 in step 25 above). This is the percentage of uncommitted office time available for self-initiated or directed crime prevention activities. As stated in **Chapter 6**, agencies with less than about 40 percent uncommitted time begin to see significantly fewer officer-initiated activities. Agencies with under 15 percent usually have little or no self-initiated activities because officers are running from one call to the next.

By now you should be able to determine the approximate percentage of patrol uncommitted time along with other statistics, such as response time, and have a good understanding of the current level of services being provided.

If your agency currently has over 40 percent patrol uncommitted time, that means your officers can manage the workload easily during the day. Sometimes officers have large blocks of time with no incoming calls. They can use that time productively; *if* that time is effectively managed and directed.

This does not mean that all officers will have the same amount of un-committed time. Different amounts of uncommitted time depend on the shift assigned, the time of day when most calls are received, the area to which they are assigned, not to mention many other factors. A good officer's daily activity report submitted daily and totaled by the supervisor quickly shows what officers are doing with their time.

If your agency has between 30-40 percent patrol uncommitted time, your officers should be able to manage time effectively to conduct proactive activities, *if* they are managed and directed appropriately. However, if your patrol uncommitted time is less than 30 percent, it is possible that your officers may have some uncommitted time. Note that this time is usually broken up into such small increments between calls that meaningful activity is unable to be performed.

If your department currently has less than 40 percent uncommitted time, and you want to know how many additional patrol officers are needed to reach the 40 percent goal, you can use this same data and enter it appropriately into the patrol staffing model (**Appendix B**) to determine the number of officers needed.

Line	Description	Input
	Computation of Current Uncommitted Time in Patrol	
	Computing Officer Total Available Time	
1	Shift length in Hours	
2	Current Call Answering Officers in Patrol	
3	Gross Paid Hours per Year	2080
4	Average Voluntary Hours Off per Officer (Vac., Hol., and Comp.)	
5	Average Sick Hours used per Officer for Previous Year	
6	Average Admin Hours (Injury, Military, Suspension, Bereavement)	
7	Average Training Hours per officer for Previous Year	
8	Average Patrol Officer Hours at Work for Year	
9	Average number of shifts each officer present for work	
10	Estimated administrative time per shift per officer	
11	Total administrative time at work per officer per year	
12	Total hours each officer doing police work each year	
13	Total Patrol Officer hours available for police work for year period	
	Computing Current Time related to Calls for Service	
14	Citizen-Generated Calls for Service Dispatched in Previous 12 Months	
15	Average Time on Call for All Calls for Service	
16	Computed Total Time on Call	
17	Number of Custody Arrests made in Previous 12 Months	
18	Estimated Average Transport and Booking Time per prisoner	
19	Computed Total Time on Prisoner related activities	
20	Total Reports Written in Previous 12 Months	
21	Estimated Average time to complete report	
22	Computed Total Time completing written reports	
23	Estimated Ancillary non-police duties in Previous Year	
24	Total Time handling Citizen Calls and Ancillary Duties	
25	Percentage of Available Officer Time handling Calls and Ancillary Duties	
26	Percentage of Available Officer Time Uncommitted	

Table 6: *This worksheet allows easy data entry and computation using the previous instructions.*

APPENDIX B: Patrol Staffing Model

This model is a simple *workload* model. It uses the same historical data gathered for use in **Appendix A** and computes the total time necessary to accomplish the required tasks. It then divides that time by the average work time available per officer to determine the total number of officers needed to meet the required service level.

This model can be used for the entire patrol force (producing the total number of patrol officers needed, not separated by shift) simply by putting the total number of citizen-generated calls in the top section. You can also use this model to determine the number of officers needed on each shift by putting the number of calls for service received on each shift.

Data entry items

Line 1: Citizen-generated calls for service dispatched in previous 12 months

Most departments assign incident numbers to every police activity, including officer-initiated activities such as traffic stops and jail checks. While this is police activity, it does not accurately indicate the citizen call service requirements. It is important that the number used here be the actual number of citizen-generated calls that were dispatched to field elements and should not include any officer-generated activity. It should not include traffic stops, jail checks, business checks, or other non-call-related activities. Many CAD systems can produce this data by selecting the call source (such as 911 or administrative line, and not the officer). If not, produce a list of all incidents in the last 12 months by type of call (such as accident, assault, burglary, and others) with the total calls of each type and a grand total. You can then identify the types of incidents that are officer-generated (such as traffic stops) and remove them from the total.

Line 2: Average on-call time for all service calls

Average time on-call is obtained from CAD data for just citizen-generated calls. Enter as a percentage of one hour. When reliable data is absent from the CAD system, use between .66 and .75. On average, most agencies' actual data for officer time on-call ranges between 40 and 45 minutes per call.

Greater Accuracy: To achieve greater accuracy for your specific agency, some CAD systems can produce the total time spent on-call for all units assigned to all calls. In most cities roughly 40-50 percent of calls require two officers, and about 6-8 percent require three or more. Some CAD systems track these times separately and can produce more accurate data regarding the total hours spent handling citizen calls. Dispatch supervisors and managers can query their systems to produce accurate data for the number of citizen-generated calls and total unit time on these calls. If the city has an IT unit, these staff members can be called upon to provide accurate data from CAD systems.

Line 3: Computed total time on-call

This is computed by multiplying line 1 by line 2. This calculation produces the total time officers spent in the previous 12 months being at the scene of citizen-generated calls for service. There are other duties required when answering citizen-generated calls, such as writing reports and booking prisoners. We can capture that time below.

Note: If the department can track overtime by cause, then the number of hours of late relief overtime due to a citizen's call for service can be added to this total. All overtime should not be added because it is being used for many other reasons.

Line 4: Number of custody arrests made in previous 12 months

This data may be provided by the CAD, records management, or jail management systems. Use the most accurate data possible and only those resulting from citizen-generated incidents for the greatest accuracy, if possible.

Line 5: Estimated average transport and booking time per prisoner

This time varies significantly between departments depending on whether they have an internal jail or must drive a prisoner to the county jail and the distances involved. Field supervisors and officers should be queried, and sample data collected from the CAD system to estimate the average. Clearly drunk driving arrests require longer booking processes due to intoxilyzer or blood draws requirements, but an accurate average can be developed using CAD data. Enter as a percent of one hour (45 minutes = .75 or an hour and a half = 1.5).

Line 6: Computed total time on prisoner-related activities

This figure is generated by multiplying line 4 by line 5. This is the total time spent on booking prisoners from citizen-generated calls.

Line 7: Total reports written in the previous 12 months

This data is obtained from the department's records management system.

Line 8: Estimated average time to complete a report

Most departments do not capture report-writing time in their CAD system. When this is the case, field supervisors and officers will need to generate this estimate. It is remarkable that in previous staffing studies within multiple agencies, the report-writing time is similar, usually 45 minutes per report or .75 of an hour. If more accurate data is not available from your CAD system, use .75.

Line 9: Computed total time completing written reports

This is computed by multiplying line 7 by line 8.

Line 10: Estimated ancillary non-police duties from the previous year

Some police agencies have their police officers doing other activities not specifically related to police work. Examples include transporting municipal court revenue to the bank, locking and unlocking city halls and libraries, performing bailiff duties in the municipal court. These activities take officers away from citizen call-answering duties as well as proactive officer-initiated and crime-prevention activities which are often overlooked by administrators. Department staff can closely estimate the total time needed to perform these activities and enter here the total number of hours spent in a year on these ancillary activities.

Line 11: Total time handling citizen calls and ancillary duties

This is computed by adding lines 3, 6, 9, and 10. Next we must determine the number of hours each patrol officer has available to contribute to handling these calls and ancillary duties.

Line 12: Shift length

Patrol shift length in the number of hours, usually 8, 10, or 12. This is used to determine how many days an officer shows up to work a patrol shift during the year.

Line 13: Gross paid hours per year

This is the total number of hours that an officer is designed to work during a year. (Usually, 26 two-week pay periods of 80 hours = 2080 hours).

Line 14: Average voluntary hours off per officer

The average number of hours from personnel time record, even if in FMLA status. Use a 12-month payroll report to tally the number of vacation, holiday and compensatory time hours taken by officers assigned to call-answering duties. Next divide this number by the number of call-answering officers to obtain the average.

Line 15: Average sick hours used per officer for previous year

The average number of hours from personnel time records, even if in

FMLA status.

Line 16: Average administrative hours off

This average comes from personnel time records and includes injury, jury duty, military leave, quarantine, death in family leave, and suspension time. In other words, all admin time that is not captured elsewhere.

Line 17: Average training hours per officer for the previous year

Average hours of training for the year for each officer including both scheduled schools and in-service training.

Line 18: Average patrol officer hours at work for the year

This is computed by subtracting lines 14, 15, 16, and 17, from line 13.

Line 19: Average number of shifts each officer is present for work.

This is computed by dividing line 18 by line 12. This is the number of shifts a patrol officer is expected to be at work during a year.

Line 20: Estimated administrative time per shift per officer

Even when an officer is at work, the entire shift is not spent doing productive police work. This is the estimate of the average amount of unrecoverable time per shift an officer uses for briefing, meals, breaks, court, vehicle maintenance, and other individual administrative activities. Usually 1.5 for 8-hour shifts, 2 for 10-hour shifts, and 2.5 for 12-hour shifts, but your department should refine these estimates based on your operation.

Line 21: Total administrative time at work per officer per year

This is computed by multiplying line 19 by line 20. This figure produces the total time an officer spends doing administrative activities. While this may not be considered *police work* that is still required or allowed) for the entire year.

Line 22: Total hours each officer doing police work each year

This figure is computed by subtracting line 21 from line 18. This is the gross paid hours minus the time off from work (vacations, holidays, sick time and training and so on) and minus the non-police administrative activities (shift briefings, meal breaks, vehicle maintenance, etc.) that are required when at work. This leaves the total amount of time the average officer has each year to conduct police work. The actual police work includes answering citizen calls and proactive officer-initiated actions. Next enter the percentage of desired proactive or uncommitted time (not answering calls or conducting ancillary duties) desired.

Line 23: Percent uncommitted/proactive time desired

Agencies should strive for a bare minimum of 20-30 percent and a minimum of 40-45 percent for effective crime control activity levels. Expressed in the formula as a decimal.

Line 24: Computed total officer time needed

This is computed by dividing Line 11 by (1 minus line 23). In other words, if the percentage of proactive time desired (line 23) is 40 percent or .40, then the computation is Line 11 divided by .60. This computes the total number of officer hours needed to answer all calls, perform all ancillary duties, and have the desired percentage of uncommitted or proactive time for officers to conduct crime control and self-initiated activities.

Line 25: Computing the number of officers required

The final number of officers required to meet this requirement is the total hours of officer time needed (Line 24), divided by the average number of hours each officer has available (Line 22).

Line	Description	Input
	PATROL STAFFING MODEL	
	Computing Time Needed for Responding to Citizen Calls and Ancillary Duties	
1	Citizen-Generated Calls for Service Dispatched in Previous 12 Months	
2	Average Time on Call for All Calls for Service	
3	Computed Total Time on Call	
4	Number of Custody Arrests made in Previous 12 Months	
5	Estimated Average Transport and Booking Time per prisoner	
6	Computed Total Time on Prisoner related activities	
7	Total Reports Written in Previous 12 Months	
8	Estimated Average time to complete report	
9	Computed Total Time completing written reports	
10	Estimated Ancillary non-police duties in Previous Year	
11	Total Time handling Citizen Calls and Ancillary Duties	
	Computing Officer Time Availability	
12	Shift length in Hours	
13	Gross Paid Hours per Year	2080
14	Average Voluntary Hours Off per Officer (Vac., Hol., and Comp.)	
15	Average Sick Hours used per Officer for Previous Year	
16	Average Admin Hours (Injury, Military, Suspension, Bereavement)	
17	Average Training Hours per officer for Previous Year	
18	Average Patrol Officer Hours at Work for Year	
19	Average number of shifts each officer present for work	
20	Estimated administrative time per shift per officer	
21	Total administrative time at work per officer per year	
22	Total hours each officer doing police work each year	
	Uncommitted Time Decision Input	
23	Percent Uncommitted/Proactive Time Desired (percent as decimal)	
24	Computed Total Officer time needed (Calls, Ancillary, and Desired Proactive)	
25	Computed Number of Officers Required	

Table 7: *This worksheet is designed to allow easy data entry and computation using the previous instructions.*

APPENDIX C: Police Monthly Reporting

City managers and councils often require police departments to make formal, periodic reports on their operations and performance. When reviewing reports from various police departments, there is great diversity in the content, format and timing of these reports. While police chiefs have the *day-to-day* responsibility for managing and controlling their police department, city managers and city councils, or their respective counterparts in other types of organizations, also have a responsibility for the department's *proper and efficient performance*. Periodic reports from the departments are the most convenient method of constant monitoring. However, reviewing periodic reports can be dangerous if it replaces asking direct questions or substitutes for personal interaction.

In most cases, it is inappropriate for elected officials to become directly involved in specific police operations or investigative cases. Neither should they be directly involved in personnel matters. However, it is impossible for them to represent the desires of their constituents properly without the ability to ask operational questions and receive accurate and timely responses. Questions like, "What training has been provided to patrol officers in the past year? Has the department received training in procedural justice? If so, how much? How many body camera audits have been completed by supervisors in the past month? What is the department doing to control crime? How many uses of force above simple handcuffing occurred, and is this up or down from last year?" Questions such as these are critical to ensuring police agencies are performing to the expectations of the citizens they serve.

It is an interesting phenomenon that both employees and organizations do what is measured. If you do not measure it, then it must not be that important. However, if you are measuring it, reporting it, and asking questions about it, then it must be important. That is one of the reasons that goal setting and strategic planning are so important. Reporting is actually a method of inspection. Thus, this old auditing adage applies: *Don't expect what you don't inspect!*

Personal visits to a department are important because it shows support for the officers and interest in what they are doing and their working conditions. An accompanied tour of the facility, an in-office visit with the chief, or a visit to the dispatch office can provide information not available from police reports.

Sitting in a patrol briefing and saying a few *words of support* can have a significant impact on the department's morale. It also allows observation of whether officers appear to support their supervisors, whether crime control strategies are being discussed, whether any training is being offered and other insights. As a courtesy, always advise the police chief and city manager in advance of any planned visits.

Periodic reports are necessary to identify emerging trends and allow corrections *before* they become major problems. These reports are needed to make sure the department is attempting to achieve the goals set by the council. So, what needs to be in these periodic reports? That will depend on the size of the city, what issues are believed to be important, and how much work it will take to collect the data. It is highly unlikely that two reports will ever be the same, but we can identify some common features. Additionally, it makes no sense to have a department go to great lengths to collect and report data if the manager or council members don't want it or don't review it. Development of any periodic reports should be an interaction between the governing body, city manager and chief of police.

Content

Content for periodic reports is dependent on the type of agency, its operational goals and strategic plan. Goals for a city government, reducing crime, answering calls for service, and managing traffic, may be significantly different from those of a school district, college, or transit police department whose goals may be to protect students or riders, the facilities, manage parking, and be prepared for critical incidents.

- Usually, content is focused on three areas: operations, personnel, and administration.

Operational data may include:

- Citizen or student-generated calls for service, possibly even identifying those with mental health-related issues

- Crimes reported, showing felony and misdemeanor.

- Traffic stops and citations

- Parking citations (if parking is a problem)

- Arrests showing felony, misdemeanor, drunk driving and others

- Accidents reported involving both injury and non-injury, as well as top accident locations

- Vehicle pursuits and results

These activities merely state what the department is *doing*. While these activities are important and need to be reported, they do not address the *results*. They don't show if the goals or objectives in the strategic plan were achieved. The performance measures we discuss here are results oriented. Again, different agencies may have different performance measures depending on their operational goals. Both activities and performance measures need to be reviewed to determine if the activities are producing the *desired results*.

- Performance measurements include:
- Crime rate, up or down, compared to a standard like last year or the state or regional average
- Citizen satisfaction, perhaps measured by periodic surveys of residents or victims
- Response time to emergency and non-emergency calls
- Clearance rate of reported crimes, perhaps by category
- Accident rate, up or down or compared to a standard

If the department is working on a special crime control program, such as hot-spot area policing or a form of focused deterrence, then reporting the activity and results within that specific project needs to be considered. Progress on the department's strategic plan also needs to be reported. Again, if it gets measured, *it gets done*.

- Personnel data may include:
- Current staffing, perhaps by unit with vacancies identified for both sworn and non-sworn personnel
- Training hours provided, including topics and class length
- Employee complaints and early intervention system activity
- Employee injuries and status
- Significant issues or accomplishments (promotions, births, awards)
- Administrative data may include:

- Type and number of internal audits performed

- Number of random body camera video reviews conducted by supervisors

- Current budget expenditures

- Overtime usage

- Equipment and facility issues

- A narrative of department status from the chief

While these are mere examples, the governmental body must first determine the goals of its police department and then design the report contents to ensure proper monitoring. The contents need to be a collaboration between the governing body or administrator and the police chief. In some agencies, gathering data for a report may be so time-consuming that it is not worth the information it provides. The chief must design or implement processes to make gathering and reporting data easy.

Even if the report takes more time than is believed to be necessary, requiring data to be collected may heighten a task's importance within an agency. This effort communicates that it is important because it allows the chief and other managers and supervisors to identify trends, then take corrective actions to achieve the agency's goals.

Format

The format for periodic reports is determined by the users. They can be a single page for smaller departments, or a multi-page report for larger departments with significantly larger and more complex operations. Parts of the report may be in narrative form and others in a tabular form. Often overlooked, however, is the inclusion of comparative data. If the department tells you that the response time is 6.4 minutes, is this good or bad? Is it up or down from last month or last year? How do you evaluate that data without keeping all the prior reports, pulling them out to compare the numbers?

Making a report easy to review and evaluate means including both the operational goal and data from the last reporting period, year-to-date numbers, the same reporting period for the previous year, and year-to-date numbers for the previous year. This allows the reviewer to identify developing trends, determine if there are seasonal variations versus last year, or if see that everything is basically the same as previous reports. Consider showing data in a two-year graph format, as shown in **Table 8.** Include data for each period graphically, in addition to tabular format. The goal is to clearly identify all the information on the graph. This visual representation is much easier to view and quicker to understand, and is a great way to recognize trends. When two years are completed, the oldest year's data is dropped, and the graph shifts to allow data entry going forward.

Table 8: This example shows the historical response time by month and the department response time goal. (2023)

Data Sample

Table 8: *This example shows the historical response time by month and the department response time goal. (2023)*

Timing

How often is enough? Again, this depends on the department's size, how difficult it is to construct the report, and the importance of certain operations. Most agencies produce some kind of monthly report for their governing body. The content of this report may be decided by a police chief who believes he or she knows what the administration needs, or what he or she wants them to see. The governing body and/or the chief administrators are ultimately responsible for the department's operation and need to ensure they receive the data they need, and at what intervals, to ensure it operates appropriately. Some police chiefs misunderstand this relationship.

There is no requirement that all data be reported at the same interval. In reality, it is much easier to gather data and create reports in smaller bites versus including everything in one report. Monthly reports may contain a certain level of data. Quarterly reports could contain additional data and analysis. Items that are time-intensive to compile may be better suited for quarterly or annual reports rather than monthly reports.

Once all relevant parties decide about content and timing to be included in the periodic report, the chief of police can then develop systems within the agency to collect the data and make the required reports. For instance, the current CAD system does not track automated report response times. Therefore, the chief needs to investigate an alternate means to compile and compute this data manually. If it becomes a difficult and time-consuming process, the chief may need to discuss the issue with the administration to determine a less burdensome method to report response times. In most cases, chiefs can require supervisors and managers within their areas of responsibility to promptly gather and report the required data. This communicates to lower-level supervisors and managers that these items are important, and that others are watching their performance.

Some larger agencies have developed automated data collection, as well as constructing and transmitting the report on a specific date. Some have even developed electronic *dashboards* to keep data current and viewable by administrators, and in some cases citizens.

APPENDIX D: Audits and Inspections

Trusting your employees to do the right thing and follow the department's policies is vital for police work. Officers and non-sworn employees often work alone and independently without direct supervision. Most officers and employees conform to the department's expectations and comply with directives. Over time, however, humans tend to find ways to do jobs easier and faster. It is a natural characteristic of humans to reduce the time and effort needed to accomplish a task. Sometimes this results in skipped steps or simply doing things another way that may increase safety risks – whether for the officer and / or the public. If the original tasks were developed to specifically reduce safety risks or reduce potential liability, skipping steps or doing things the wrong way can have devastating consequences.

While trusting your employees is necessary, conducting audits and inspections is a significant part of monitoring performance and supervision in any organization. One of the first questions raised in police auditing classes is, "What needs to be audited?" The answer is anything that can cause the agency problems. An exercise in many auditing classes is to conduct a risk assessment. Using a matrix with high-to-low risk and frequent-to-rare occurrences helps to identify items or processes that pose the most risk to your agency and, therefore, should be at the top of the list for items to be audited. Many high-risk activities, even those with an exceptionally low occurrence rate, for example an active shooter incident, need to be audited for proper policy, training, necessary equipment and response procedures.

In most cases, police departments can conduct their own internal audits. However, in some circumstances, organizations may be needed to provide outside expertise. This *outside assistance* can come from other police agencies, city or organizational units, or even consulting companies. Asking an outside organization what can go wrong can help identify specific auditing needs.

Conducting risk analysis specific to the organization and department will clearly produce numerous areas for effective audits and inspections. To assist in this process, the audits listed below may provide a starting point. Based on years of experience, police agencies across the country have had significant problems with these issues. The suggested audits are ranked based on the following five-point scale:

Five Point Scale:

- 5   High risk to physical safety of officers or citizens.

- 4   High risk to department reputation, community trust, or ability to prosecute offenders.

- 3   Medium risk to department reputation, community trust, or ability to prosecute offenders.

- 2   Lower risk, but needed to ensure integrity of department and public trust.

- 1   Low risk, but needed to ensure appropriate internal operations and relationships.

- X   Dependent on nature of complaint.

Not all suggested audits are necessary in every organization, nor will this be a complete list. Agencies with different goals for their police department most likely will benefit from other audits.

Department policies and operations	
Department policies for critical activities	5
Use of force policy and training	5
Department policy updating and receipt process	4
Compliance with civil rights policies	4
Body worn camera usage	4
Off-duty job process	3
Community engagement	3
CJIS requirements	3
Hiring and selection process	3
Promotional process	2
Whistleblower complaints	X
Specific incident analysis	X
Community/council complaints	X
Department facilities and equipment	
Officer equipment and weapons	5
Department owned firearms	4
Department owned tracking devices	4
Department owned less-lethal weapons	3
Department equipment/database use	3

Ammunition tracking and use	2
Vehicle maintenance and fuel costs	2
Capital assets	2
Radar gun accuracy and calibration	2
Disaster recovery preparations	2
Vehicle usage and needs	1
Vehicle emergency equipment	1
Facility inspection	1
Internal affairs	
Personnel complaint process	5
Personnel commendation process	4
IA and internal investigation process	4
Use of force reporting and investigation	4
Early Intervention System operation	4
IA files security	3
Employees on Facebook/social media	3
Annual complaint analysis process	3
Worker's compensation audit	2
Officer involved critical incident investigation process	2
Car-to-car, phone messaging	2
Patrol/enforcement and bias prevention	
Vehicle pursuits and reports	5
Traffic stops and citations	5
Racial profiling (cites by officer by race)	4
Arrests for penalty offenses (by race)	4
Arrest report accuracy	4
Supervisory response to field incidents	4
Citations by type (by officer)	3
Arrests by charge (by officer)	3
Compliance with procedural justice	3
Sexual assault investigation process	3
Supervisory review of body camera video	3
Report writing	3
Department staffing and response time	3
Investigative units	
Critical case follow-up (special victims)	4
Search warrant applications and affidavits	4
Investigative unit case files	3
Criminal intelligence files and searches	3

118

DA case report requirements	3
Supervisory case management	3
Evidence analysis and case backlogs	2
Audio and video recording procedures	2
Jail/detentions operations	
Jail/booking intake and operations	5
Jail facility security and operations	5
Prisoner property/medical/rights compliance	5
Property and evidence	
Property and evidence security and inventory	4
Destruction of firearms	2
Destruction of narcotics	2
Disposal process	2
Impounded vehicles	2
Files and records	
Training status (TCOLE requirements)	3
Personnel files – TCOLE requirements	2
Traffic citation security	2
UCR/NIBERS reporting process	2
Performance evaluations	1
Financial	
Cash receipts and accounting	4
Confidential funds	4
Regular overtime approval, use and reporting	3
Special grants overtime	3
Petty cash	3
Travel expenses	3
Purchasing equipment/services	3
Timesheets and time reporting	2
Sick and comp time usage	2
Specialized units	
Special operations units	5
SWAT operations and training	5
High-risk warrant execution process	5
Street crimes unit operations	5
Gang unit operations	5
Specialized unit training	5
Crime scene forensic collection and processing	4

Review of critical incidents – after action reports	3
Narcotics Operations	
Narcotics operational procedures and controls	5
Confiscated/forfeited drug money	4
Drug buy money/ confidential funds	4
Confidential informant files and controls	4
Deconfliction process	4
Training drugs for K-9	3

Table 9: *List of suggested audits and inspections with relative level of importance. (2023)*

www.ingramcontent.com/pod-product-compliance
Lightning Source LLC
Chambersburg PA
CBHW080421030426
42335CB00020B/2533